WRITING
LOVE
SCENES

by Rayne Hall
and Susanne McCarthy

WRITING LOVE SCENES

by Rayne Hall and Susanne McCarthy

Book cover by Erica Syverson and Manuel Berbin

© 2018 Rayne Hall

March 2018 Edition

ISBN-13: 978-1547280742

ISBN-10: 1547280743

British English.

TABLE OF CONTENTS

INTRODUCTION

Do you want to write powerful love scenes which stir the reader's emotions?

This book shows you how to create a vivid love scene or improve a bland draft so it touches the reader's heart. You will learn the techniques professional authors use to create conflict, depth and intensity, and craft heart-warming and harrowing scenes that stay forever in the reader's mind.

We – dark fiction author and creator of the Writer's Craft series Rayne Hall, and romance author Susanne McCarthy – have combined our expertise and will show you how to write love scenes like a pro.

Whether you pen romance novels or need a compelling love scene for a different genre, this book is for you.

Some chapters are useful for all fiction genres, for example, how to write flirtatious dialogue and how to describe a romantic location. Others serve specific plot situations, such as first kiss, characters in disguise, confessing a secret, break-ups and marriage proposals.

In some sections, we provide guidance for specific kinds of fiction, such as how to write gay love scenes or relationships between different species. You decide which topics are relevant for your writing, and select which chapters you want to study.

Depending on how steamy or chaste you want your love scenes, we offer you a menu of topics to choose from: writing graphic sex, implying sex without showing it, creating erotic tension without erotic action, and keeping love scenes chaste. Select the ones that suit your taste and the kind of story you write.

At the end of each chapter, we give you assignments, so you can put what you've learned into practice and take your novel-in-progress forward.

You won't find 'rules' here. Instead of telling you what and how to write, we reveal our professional techniques and show you how to apply them. You choose which of our pieces of advice you want to use in your writing.

We – Rayne and Susanne – write differently. That's why Susanne has added suggestions to Rayne's chapters, and Rayne to Susanne's. The different perspectives will inspire your own creative choices and enhance your individual author voice.

We assume that you've mastered the foundations of the fiction writing craft, and that you know how to write basic dialogue, develop characters and build a plot. If you're a novice just starting out, it may be best to set this book aside for now and start with a beginner-level guide to fiction writing. Our book is for writers who are ready to master specialised skills.

Like all books in the Writer's Craft series, this guide focuses in depth on one specific topic: how to write love scenes. It doesn't cover story structure and novel plotting.

We both use British English, so if you're used to American English, some words and spellings may look unfamiliar. To avoid convoluted phrases of the 'he or she does this to her or him' type, we use the female pronoun in some sections and the male in others.

Now let's get started and create the love scenes your novel's characters deserve.

Rayne Hall & Susanne McCarthy

CHAPTER 1

WHAT MAKES A GOOD LOVE SCENE?

Rayne Hall

Two people enjoying each other's company in comfortable surroundings, saying 'I love you' and feeling happy with not a cloud on the horizon... in real life, that's a wonderful experience. But it makes a boring love scene.

Adding sex doesn't guarantee an exciting scene. Indeed, many great love scenes don't feature intimate action. Love is a feeling, and your job as a writer is to let your readers share in what the story characters feel. How can you achieve that?

SIX CRUCIAL INGREDIENTS

1. **The scene keeps the characters apart.** I can almost hear you saying "What?! Surely love scenes are about the couple being close?" But if the characters are united in every sense, the scene is static, the love story is over, and the reader is bored. Find a way to keep the characters from being fully united. For example, they may be physically close (holding each other in a tight embrace) but know that they may never meet again. Or perhaps they are with other people, and although they manage to signal their love, they must be careful that nobody else guesses their secret betrothal.

2. **The scene has conflict.** Conflict doesn't mean arguments! Experienced fiction writers know that conflict drives readers to keep reading. A good scene has both inner and outer conflicts. For guidance on how to layer conflicts in a love scene, see the chapter 'Inner, Outer and Relationship Conflicts'.

3. **The scene takes the relationship in a new direction.** Something changes between the two. Perhaps they learn to trust each other more – or maybe the opposite happens, and they trust each other less. They may be more confident about a shared future than before – or their plans for their life together collapse. They are more committed to each other than before – or perhaps one of them withdraws from the commitment.

4. **The scene takes the whole story in a new direction.** Every scene in your book changes the direction of the plot, ideally in ways the reader didn't expect. Twists and turns make the story exciting to read. Love scenes are no exception.

5. **The scene grabs the reader emotionally.** Whether your scene is heart-warming or heart-wrenching, it must do something to the reader's heart. The reader needs to feel what the characters feel – not just love, but the whole mix of emotions the characters go through, such as desire, despair, yearning, hurt, jealousy, trust, gratitude and hope. For tips on how to create reader emotion, see the chapter 'How to Stir the Reader's Emotions'.

6. **The Point-of-View Character grows as a result of the scene.** She will probably be wiser in some way. Perhaps she'll be more cautious or more courageous, bolder or calmer. The other lover who is not the PoV probably changes too, although their growth may be less obvious to the reader. (For more about this, see the chapter 'How to Immerse the Reader: Point-of-View'.)

WHAT NOT TO DO

Novice writers tend to write love scenes in which both characters are happy, rejoicing in their love, and enjoying their togetherness, with no problem or conflict. Don't bore your readers.

Don't write a static love scene in which nothing changes. The scene needs to alter the character, the relationship and the direction of the story.

SUSANNE'S SUGGESTION

"A good love story has two characters whom the reader is rooting for – because they are attractive (though not necessarily beautiful), likable, perhaps noble. The reader knows they should be together, wants them to be together – but something is keeping them apart. That something should be significant, or the book will end up sailing across the room.

Each love scene within the story will be a microcosm of that tension between attraction and conflict. Each scene should nudge the story forward – though the balance between attraction and conflict may vary, and sometimes it will seem to take the story backwards if conflict appears to be winning.

Therefore each scene should be carefully placed on the arc of the story to ensure that the progression is meaningful, that it doesn't go round in circles, that it doesn't make irrational leaps or depend on awkward contrivances.

Each scene should increase the tension, until the story reaches its climax, when attraction and conflict explode – and hopefully attraction wins (though not always with a Happy-Ever-After if you are not writing for the Romance market.)"

ASSIGNMENT

Think about a love scene you want to write for your novel, or read a draft you've written. Which of those six ingredients does it have, and which are still lacking?

Decide which ingredients you still need to add or want to strengthen.

You can then use this book to help fix those 'problem areas'.

CHAPTER 2

CHARACTERS – UNDERSTANDING THE LOVERS

Susanne McCarthy

Who are these people you have created? What are their personality traits? Are they shy or confident, bold or awkward, charming, persuasive, caring? Is he rich and powerful, and accustomed to getting his own way – or maybe he's a senior officer in the Sindril Guard, and when he says "jump" everyone jumps? Is he a doctor, a paramedic, a police officer, always putting the needs of other people first?

How physically attractive are they – how does that affect how people react to them? And how do they rate their own looks? The raving beauty who doesn't think she's even pretty is a bit of an irritating cliché – but maybe there's something slightly quirky about her looks (think of the actress Julia Roberts, who starred in the film *Pretty Woman*. Her mouth is wa-a-ay too wide for her face, but when she smiles…!) Or maybe she downplays her looks because she wants to be taken seriously in her profession.

What about their back-story – their childhood experiences, their family, their previous romantic entanglements? Maybe she had an unstable childhood, a mother who drank, an absent father, a series of foster homes. That may have made her very independent and self-contained, wary of getting involved with anyone. When she feels herself getting too close to someone, she may back off in alarm.

Or maybe her parents had a very happy marriage, and she wants that for herself – but she can't see this workaholic businessman or reckless Sindril warrior as being suitable material.

Have they had a previous heartbreak – a broken affair, a divorce? They may be reluctant to trust a new lover, they may project onto them their previous experiences – her fiancé was unfaithful and she is afraid of that happening again, suspicious of other women in his life. His first wife was after his money – any little suggestion that this new woman has similar ambitions will be magnified in his mind. And that's going to apply tenfold if the previous lover or spouse is the one who has come back into their life now.

If he's a grieving widower, he'll mentally compare the new love interest with the remembered perfection of his late wife. If he comes from a society where women are seen as subordinate to men, he'll expect to take the lead in the relationship. If he is chaste, he'll discourage her seduction attempts and distance himself from her because he thinks she isn't good wife material.

Then there's the anti-hero, who can be male or female – the bad boy can be a real charmer, the bitch can be fatally attractive. He (or she) is an intriguing mix of good and bad – he does have some moral standards but they will tend to be his own, only matching society's standards by chance. He will probably have serious flaws, but doesn't feel bad about them – he will minimise them or laugh at society's disapproval.

He is likely to be expert in the game of seduction, and to have few scruples about how he wins. This is going to set up considerable internal conflict for his target. The attraction is powerful, but she knows he is dangerous. When he has done something good and noble she will lower her guard, only to snap it back into place when he does something reprehensible. And all the time she's hoping that the love of a good woman will redeem him – and maybe it will. (This is, after all, fiction.)

Think also about the fundamental differences between your characters, and the impact that will have – for example, differences in wealth and social class. In the chapter 'Different Cultures,

Different Species' we discuss the impact of cultural, religious and even species differences, as well as the impact of racism.

HOW DOES CHARACTER IMPACT ON LOVE SCENES?

You will have fed some of this back-story into your tale, enough so that their present behaviour makes some kind of sense to your readers. Now you need to consider how these factors will influence the way you present your love scenes. Everything about your characters, their personality traits and their back-story, will affect where you place the love scenes in your story, and how each scene will play out.

Whether or not one or both of your lovers is new to this or has plenty of experience will affect how they react to each other as the tension escalates, how they initiate or respond to kisses, to love-making. An experienced lover will tend to be more confident, although the strength of the attraction to his partner, how significant this relationship is to him, may unsettle him. A confident lover may move in for a kiss much sooner than a young lad who's only kissed one girl before, behind the bike sheds. And the confident lover will get the moves right, while the callow lad will worry about what to do – how do you keep your nose from getting in the way when you're kissing?

Much of the conflict between them will arise from character – see the sections on 'First Impressions' and 'Fighting the Attraction'. As circumstances force them to be together, the affair will progress in fits and starts – each scene which shows progress will be followed by a reaction. One minute he is brusque and cold, then he kisses her – then he is even colder. Which confuses her and makes her angry – this will heighten the tension in each scene between the physical attraction and mental resistance.

WHAT TO AVOID

When your characters are in conflict, be careful not to make the love scenes too repetitive. Shade each scene to move them along their story arc. But don't make the progression too smooth and predictable: Looking > brief kiss > steamier kiss > some fondling… Shake it up a little – maybe that first kiss is *very* steamy, but then they have to go back to square one.

RAYNE'S SUGGESTION

"Write your love scene so it can happen only between those two characters. Everything they say, feel, think and do must fit their personalities. Is there any part in the love scene where you could replace the characters with someone else, and it would still unfold in the same way? Then it's not good enough. Rewrite that section."

FURTHER STUDY

If you want to explore characterisation in depth, consider the book *Writing Vivid Characters* from the Writer's Craft series.

ASSIGNMENT

Write a paragraph which tells the reader three things about your character solely through the way they kiss.

CHAPTER 3

HOW TO IMMERSE THE READER: POINT-OF-VIEW

Rayne Hall

Get deep into one character's head and heart, and let the reader experience the whole scene from this perspective. The reader practically becomes that character, and becomes deeply emotionally involved.

Which character should you choose for the Point-of-View (PoV)?

If you tell the whole story from a single character's perspective, then stick to this PoV for the love scene as well. If you write the story alternating between two or more perspectives, then here are some pointers for choosing the best PoV for this scene.

THE IDEAL POV

1. The character is present throughout the scene. If one of the lovers arrives late, perhaps after the other has already interacted with other people, or leaves early, then she wouldn't be a good choice.

2. The character has a lot at stake. This means he desperately needs something, and tries to achieve it during the scene.

3. The character's attitude to the relationship changes drastically during the scene.

4. The character undergoes a complex emotional journey during this scene, and it would be difficult to convey the subtleties without showing what goes on in her mind.

MALE AND FEMALE POINT-OF-VIEW

Did you know that women can recognise far more facial expressions than men, and are more aware of subtle expressions of emotion in the face? Men, on the other hand, are better at noticing and interpreting posture shifts. (Delving deeper into the issue would exceed the scope of this book, but if you're interested, you may want to Google the topic to find out about the scientific research.)

For a writer, this knowledge is useful, because it helps you make the PoV authentic. When writing from the woman's PoV, show the lover's facial expressions, because she notices those. If the PoV is male, write about the lover's posture shifts, because that's what he'll observe.

Of course, these differences apply to the average man and woman. Not everyone is the same. Your individual characters may be different.

CHANGING POV IN MID-SCENE

If at all possible, stick to one Point-of-View for the whole scene. Each PoV change jolts the reader out of the experience, and that's not a good thing to happen in the middle of a love scene. The best time to switch PoV is when a new scene begins.

If you absolutely must change the PoV from Character A to Character B in the middle of the scene, here is a technique to limit the 'jolt':

Finish the paragraph in A's perspective. Then write a paragraph that is perspective-neutral, neither A nor B, perhaps describing the weather or the furniture. The next paragraph is in B's Point-of-View.

WHAT NOT TO DO

Don't change the Point-of-View in the middle of a scene unless you have a compelling reason, and never switch in the middle of a paragraph.

Here's an example of a badly handled PoV switch:

> *John gazed into her emerald green eyes, and his chest filled with love. He wondered if this was the right moment to ask her to become his wife. He tried to speak, but his throat clogged. Mary's heart thudded because she could see that John was trying to speak, and she sensed that it was something important.*

SUSANNE'S SUGGESTION

"In the Romance genre, the female PoV is usually predominant. You may choose not to adopt the man's PoV at all, keeping his thoughts as much a secret from the reader as they are from your female character.

Or, include his thoughts. This comment from a reviewer of my novel *Summer Scandal* sums it up:

> *I really liked this hero because the author gave glimpses of his inner thoughts every now & again. By revealing his thought processes we see a man – used to superficial sexual relationships with women – falling in love with the heroine's sense of humour and warm personality. In this way, the reader is able to see past his hard, arrogant exterior. It humanised him."*

FURTHER STUDY

At the end of this book, I've included an excerpt from one of my novels, showing how I've handled a PoV switch between two scenes.

If you want to study this subject in more depth, you may want to look at my book *Writing Deep Point of View,* also in the Writer's Craft series.

ASSIGNMENT

Decide which character's PoV is best for this scene.

Close your eyes, and imagine the scene playing out through that character's perspective. What does she see, hear, think, feel? Pay special attention to the other lover's body language, either the facial expressions or the posture shifts.

CHAPTER 4

INNER, OUTER AND RELATIONSHIP CONFLICTS

Rayne Hall

Every fiction scene needs conflict – preferably both inner and outer conflict. Without conflict, scenes are dull and not worth reading. Love scenes are no exception.

When plotting a love scene, think of three types of conflict:

- The outer conflict (couple versus outer world)

- The relationship conflict (their goals are not compatible)

- The inner conflict (dilemma in the PoV character's heart and mind)

Technically, the relationship conflict is a form of outer conflict, but in love scenes, it's useful to treat it as a separate layer.

Examples:

1. Mary and John are in love, but they belong to different religions. Defying the wishes of his church elders, John continues to court Mary, and he visits her in her home. (Outer conflict.) John wants to stay chaste until marriage. But Mary wants to have sex. She tries hard to seduce him, while he tries to resist. (Relationship conflict.) John loves Mary, but her wanton behaviour makes him wonder if she is the right wife for him. (Inner conflict.)

2. Mary and John are in love, but their parents have arranged different marriages for them. (Outer conflict.) Mary insists on

meeting in secret, because she fears that her parents, if they discover the tryst, will immediately marry her off to the man of their choice. John, on the other hand, wants them to be open about their love. (Relationship conflict.) When John insists that he will go to her parents and demand her hand in marriage, even though she begs him not to, Mary wonders if she has made the right choice, entrusting her future to a man who takes foolish risks and disregards her wishes. (Inner conflict.)

3. Mary and John are fleeing through the jungle, hunted by savage killers. They shelter in a cave, careful not to attract attention to their hiding place. (Outer conflict.) When they get thirsty, John insists that it is he who should risk his life and venture outside at night to get water. Mary, an ardent feminist, refuses to accept the traditional roles of the male as the brave protector and the female as the helpless damsel. (Relationship conflict.) In grave danger, and not knowing whether they will survive, John yearns to tell her of his love. But she is married to another man, and marriage is sacred to John. He doesn't want to tempt Mary or himself into breaking her marriage vows. (Inner conflict.)

Your love scene doesn't need to have all three types of conflict, but should have at least two.

WHAT NOT TO DO

Don't write a scene without conflict, or with only one type of conflict.

Don't think that 'conflict' equals 'argument'. Even in the relationship conflict, the couple don't need to argue at all.

SUSANNE'S SUGGESTION

"Conflict can arise from misunderstandings. Maybe one of your characters has been misinformed about the other (possibly maliciously.) Or they make assumptions based on stereotypes (he's rich so he'll be selfish, he's good looking so he's only into casual relationships.) Or maybe they knew each other in the past – were even lovers before – and things ended badly.

But be careful to ensure that the misunderstanding is serious enough to warrant the level of conflict between them now. If it's something that could be easily resolved by one of them saying, "Hang on a minute," it's going to be very irritating for your readers.

And if someone else is being malicious, you need to ensure both that they have sufficient motive for their behaviour, and that the person being lied to has sufficient reason to believe them. Sometimes the lies may be quite subtle, just hints which play on something the listener is already unsure about.

So in these scenes there will be anger, suspicion. Her dialogue may be evasive, there may be awkward silences, visceral reactions. She is watching him closely, trying to second-guess his thoughts. He may be completely unaware that there's a problem, or maybe he's a little puzzled, trying to put right what he doesn't understand is wrong."

ASSIGNMENT

Identify the conflicts in scene. Do you have either an outer conflict or a relationship conflict (or both), as well as an inner conflict?

If a layer of conflict is missing, add it. If one of the conflicts is weak, revise it to make it more compelling.

CHAPTER 5

LOVERS TALKING: DIALOGUE

Rayne Hall

Dialogue in love scenes does more than convey whispered sweet nothings. It needs to carry the plot forward, create or resolve conflict, and develop or change the relationship in some way. Here are some professional techniques.

DIFFERENT 'VOICES'

Let the two characters speak in distinctly different ways, emphasising their contrasting personalities and backgrounds. For example, the professor will probably talk in more complex sentences and with a wider vocabulary than the farmer, and the Scot may use different words than the American.

By giving each character a distinct voice, you allow the reader to 'hear' who is talking, and don't need to clutter the scene with 'he said' and 'she said'.

BODY LANGUAGE

When newly in love, people gaze at the object of their affection a lot and observe facial expression and posture shifts far more than they ordinarily would.

A couple in an established relationship are familiar with their partner's habitual reactions, and notice immediately if something is out of the ordinary – a sudden movement, an unusual facial expression, a change in skin colour, a posture shift, a different timbre in their voice.

You can use this hyper-awareness and show a lot of body language. This way, the Point-of-View character (and through her, the reader) gets strong clues about what the other person feels.

Use different types of body language:

- Visceral reactions. *(Her throat tightened. His heart thudded.)*

- Gestures. *(She crossed her arms over her chest. He pointed at the door.)*

- Posture shifts. *(She straightened and squared her chin. He shrank back into his chair.)*

- Facial expressions. *(Her lips tightened into hard line. The corners of his eyes crinkled.)*

- Sound of voice. *(The words came out as a whisper. He spoke in a toneless voice that betrayed no emotion.)*

Use visceral reactions only for the Point-of-View character (the person through whom the reader experiences the scene) because only she is aware of those physical sensations.

The other four types serve mostly for the non-PoV character, seen through the PoV's eyes.

Using body language is another way to avoid excessive 'he said, she asked'-type tagging. Simply place the body language clue before what the character says. (In the case of sound of voice, put it after what the character says.)

He leaned forward. "Are you sure?"
She tugged at her earlobe. "Are you sure?"
My heart thudded in my throat. "Are you sure?"
"Are you sure?" Her voice sounded hoarse.

FLIRTATIOUS BANTER

When two characters become aware of their attraction for each other, but are unsure of the other's inclinations, and perhaps not ready to admit it to themselves, they test the ground by flirting.

They compliment, they tease, they hint... and everything they say can either have a flirtatious or an innocuous meaning. This way, if the other doesn't respond positively, they can always pretend they didn't mean to flirt, or that they were merely joking. These exchanges often use double entendre and sparkling wit.

Let's say Mary and John are old friends who share an interest in art. John hopes to take their relationship further, but doesn't want to risk their friendship with too bold a move. While they're visiting an art gallery, he injects a note of flirtation.

Mary studied the goddess sculpture. "Such harmony of form, such elegance and dignity. Isn't this beauty divine?"

"Indeed. I wonder why I've never realised it before."

"You've seen this statue before? I thought this was the first day of the exhibition."

He gazed into her eyes. "Is there a statue?"

If she blushes, giggles, and responds with a similar implied compliment, he'll know that she's open to romance. But if she says, *"John, don't be silly,"* he can pretend that he was only joking, and their platonic friendship will continue as before.

Clothes can be a useful conversation topic for a first cautious flirtation, because they are at the same time neutral objects and highly personal items.

Let's again take old friends Mary and John. This time, it's Mary who is looking to initiate romance. A woman can compliment and advise a male friend on his clothes, so her opening gambit is safe.

Since his response is positive, she becomes bolder and follows with more personal comments.

"That's a great shirt you're wearing. The green suits you well."

"Thanks. I was wondering if you would like it. Green is a rather bold colour, and I didn't want to be too bold for your taste."

"Oh, I like bold and green is my favourite colour. You should wear green more often. It sets off your eyes, and your tan."

"Then I'll be bold and wear green again when we meet next time. Dinner tonight at the Italian place?" He brushed a kiss on her hand. "Will you wear red for me?"

Here are some reasons why characters may use flirtation for cautious probing instead of charging ahead:

- He doesn't want to risk losing her trust or jeopardising their platonic friendship

- They belong to different ranks. He doesn't want to get fired from his job for making an unwelcome pass at his boss

- They belong to the same gender. He doesn't want to cause offence

- They are opponents or enemies and not supposed to even like each other

- She ended their relationship years ago. He doesn't want harass his ex

I'm sure you can think of further situations, including several fitting your story plot.

Readers love this banter, the probing, the teasing, the delicious uncertainty. Use the opportunity to insert flirtatious dialogue where the plot allows, and entertain your readers.

A hint of flirtation woven into an argument scene can be especially fun to read. If this would suit your story, go for it.

Craft the exchanges carefully, revising them until they sparkle. Increase the teasing humour by pruning out unnecessary words. Tight writing works best in this context, although you can insert a confused or embarrassed reaction such as... "oh" "I, ahem...", or even a stuttered, "You're... That's kind of... I mean..." reaction.

Include some funny one-liners that contain meaning, innuendo, retort and humour at the same time. I can't give examples since they arise from the situation the characters are in. Be creative, and when you come up with a one-line zinger, refine it until it sizzles.

SAYING "I LOVE YOU"

When a character says this, he is committing himself. The moment the words are spoken, the relationship changes.

Delay the moment when those words are spoken. The emotional tension grows the longer the reader has to wait.

Give the character a reason for not saying "I love you" sooner. Here are some ideas:

- He's not certain about his feelings

- His feelings are inappropriate (e.g. because she belongs to a different class, or is married)

- He worries about her reaction

- He doesn't want to make himself vulnerable

- He doesn't want to complicate or ruin a good platonic friendship

- He doesn't want to burden her with the knowledge of what he feels

- He doesn't get a chance to talk with her in private

Why does he say it now? He probably chooses the right time and place. (What makes the time and place right?) On the other hand, he may simply not be able to hold his feelings back any longer.

Insert a sentence of body language before the declaration. This will add meaning and convey emotion:

> *He cleared his throat. "I love you."*
> *She brushed a finger across his cheek. "I love you."*
> *He clasped her hands in his. "I love you."*
> *Her heart thudded in her throat. "I love you."*

Does the other person feel the same? Does she return his affections? Does she say "I love you too?"

Perhaps she likes him, or fancies him, but doesn't feel love. In this case, she may say something else nice, either letting him down gently or encouraging him to court her.

If she doesn't want his love, she may pretend not to take it seriously, play it down, or ignore what he said.

Keep the reader in suspense about how the other character will react to the declaration of love. Delay her response. Let her do something before she gives her reply – e.g. arrange the flowers, wipe the wine spill off the table – because this will heighten the suspense and make the moment exciting.

WHAT NOT TO DO

Don't let a character declare his love the moment he feels it, and don't let the other respond immediately.

Avoid two characters talking in the same 'voice'.

SUSANNE'S SUGGESTION

"There may be times when your couple are forced to spend time together, but the tension between them makes for an uneasy atmosphere. This may be in the early stages of their relationship, when there is mistrust between them or one or both of them is fighting their attraction, or it may be later when a critical point of conflict is brewing.

For example:

- Eating – in a restaurant, or at a dinner party

- Dancing

- Travelling – walking, in a car, on horseback (or dragonback!)

You can make the dialogue deliberately stilted here, with brief and banal comments: "Yes." "That's nice." In between, there may be long awkward pauses. You can describe what your PoV character is thinking and feeling, but avoid too much repetition of this.

Instead, you can illustrate the silences:

- A taut silence stretched between them

- Another long pause

- She sought for a neutral topic of conversation

- He really wasn't helping this conversation

You could also have your PoV character focus in minute detail on something trivial – the pattern on the tablecloth, a bumblebee dancing among the roses, the white streaks of cloud drifting across the sky like sweepings of a careless broom.

From my novel *Summer Scandal*:

> *Annis would have preferred to hide away at a corner table, but Theo had steered her instead to one beside the window that looked out over the rain-soaked garden, now spangled with diamonds as the bright spring sunshine reappeared from behind the clouds, sparkling on the droplets of water clinging to the grass."*

FURTHER STUDY

If you want to master dialogue writing to a high level, my book *Writing Vivid Dialogue* shows many professional techniques.

ASSIGNMENTS

1. Write a section when the two characters become aware of their attraction and probe the other's inclination with teasing flirtatious dialogue.

2. Write a section in which one character says "I love you." Delay the other's reaction in some way. Use body language to show emotion.

CHAPTER 6

CHOOSING THE LOCATION

Rayne Hall

Where does the scene take place? The location serves to put your characters – and your readers – in the right mood.

Here are three options. Which of them suits your scene?

1. A COSY SPACE

Create the image of a comfortable nest or a safe heaven. For example, you can place the couple in a cosily heated cabin while the outside the winter storms batter the walls and rattle the shutters. Psychologically, a fire creates a sense of warmth and safety, so if it suits your story, let your characters huddle around a camp fire, or relax by a log fire.

This 'cosy space' technique works especially well if the two characters don't realise yet that they're meant to be together (perhaps they're just friends, or a divorced couple), but you want the reader to sense that these two are meant for each other.

2. DRAMA

For a dramatic, memorable love scene, choose a 'wild' location: a windswept moor, a wave-lashed seashore, a craggy mountain beneath a lightning-streaked sky.

This kind of location intensifies the experience for the characters and the readers. The scene will stick in the reader's mind long after they have finished the book.

3. ENFORCED CLOSENESS

To bring two characters closer together than they would normally choose, place them in a dangerous location. Now they have to cooperate in order to be safe. This shows that they are a perfect team when it counts. They realise it, and the readers realise it too.

Professional authors use this method to drive the plot and the relationship development forward at the same time. It works especially well for characters who detest each other. Forcing them to work as a team to survive creates a delicious situation which readers will savour.

It's also great for characters who used to be in a relationship and now try to avoid each other. In the dangerous situation, they remember and cherish the other's dependability, courage and skill.

What kind of dangerous setting could you write about? Let your imagination run wild, and choose something that suits the plot: an earthquake, a blizzard, a fragile rope bridge across a chasm, a burning tower, a sinking ship...

SENSORY IMPRESSIONS

If you want the couple to have sex, prepare them – and the reader – for it by creating sensory impressions of their surroundings.

Describe sounds, smells and tactile sensations. Show how the grass (or the bathroom tiles, the fleece rug, the wooden planks, the sand) feel under her bare feet, describe the cool smoothness of the satin sheets, the sound of the water pouring into the bathtub, the smells of beeswax furniture polish and the potted geraniums.

This heightens the reader's sensory awareness, in preparation for the erotic experience. Think of it as engaging the reader in foreplay.

However, avoid unpleasant smells, because stinks kill the mood.

For an erotic scene, you don't need to give your couple perfect comfort. Rather, let them adapt to uncomfortable surroundings.

Make them squeeze into the cramped space, force them to seek shade in the blistering heat, let them feel the hard planks under their buttocks.

Unusual locations – a vegetable cellar, a private library, a cable car or a rowing boat – can increase the scene's sexiness.

WHAT NOT TO DO

New writers often believe that the setting of a love scene has to be romantic, so they evoke a palm-fringed sandy beach at sunset or a restaurant with tuxedoed waiters and a violin orchestra. But such settings are unoriginal and easily forgotten.

To make your scene memorable, choose an unusual location.

SUSANNE'S SUGGESTION

"Your couple may be at the home of one of them – her fabulous apartment overlooking Manhattan, his remote castle. But if they're going to make love, it doesn't have to be in the bedroom. Consider the bathroom, the banqueting table, the stairs... (but beds are OK.)"

FURTHER STUDY

If you want to learn more about this subject, the book *Writing Vivid Settings* from the Writer's Craft series will teach you professional techniques.

ASSIGNMENTS

1. What kind of setting would suit your scene best? Consider the three options, and choose a specific location.

2. Draw on your personal experiences of similar places. Have you ever been on a wave-lashed beach or on a windswept moor? Close your eyes and recall what detail you can.

3. If it's practical, visit a place that resembles the location and take plenty of notes, especially about sounds, smells and tactile perceptions.

CHAPTER 7

FIRST IMPRESSIONS

Susanne McCarthy

When your characters are going to fall in love, their first meeting is critical. It may occur literally as the first time they encounter each other, or maybe they have known each other in the past, when they were young – maybe they've even been lovers before, or been married. It may be that they have heard about the other person before and have already formed an opinion – possibly negative.

However you choose to approach it, their first meeting will set things up. They may be alone, or there may be other people around, but their focus on each other will be intense. They will notice details about eyes, smile, hair, body shape.

Then they will tend to notice things like how they carry themselves, how confident they appear, how they interact with other people. They will form opinions, they will have a reaction.

They will also notice whether the other person has noticed them, and may speculate on what they are thinking. Think of that moment in *Gone with the Wind*, the first time Rhett and Scarlett notice each other at the barbecue at Twelve Oaks – she says, "Who is that man? He looks as if he knows what I look like under my chemise."

It may be that one or both of them will feel an instant and powerful sexual attraction. She may feel herself blush, her body may react as if he is caressing her. That may embarrass her, puzzle her, shock her. He may feel equally frustrated by his body's overt response – as if he was still a hormone-riddled adolescent unable to control his libido.

They would also each bring their own history to this moment – their family history, their past relationships, their anxieties. But don't get too bogged down in back-story at this point – your focus should be on their thoughts and reactions in the here and now. Set them off on their adventure – and later, as they begin to get to know each other, telling each other something of their history will bring them closer.

In my novel *Summer Scandal*, Theo Lander has returned home after being away for several years. He and Annis encounter each other at her father's funeral:

He hadn't changed much, Annis noted, studying him covertly from behind the fine black veil which covered her eyes. His hair was cut rather shorter now, but that had done little to civilise him. Nor had the well-cut black cashmere overcoat he was wearing. Even from this distance she could recognise its quality.

He must have done pretty well for himself since he had left Ridgely, she mused dispassionately, in spite of the scandal which had sent his father to prison. But there was still that intriguing hint of danger about him.

She became aware that he was watching her, and was suddenly glad that she had chosen to wear a hat with a veil, though it had seemed a little over-the-top when she had first tried it on. He was still standing by himself, one hand thrust deep into the pocket of his overcoat, apparently oblivious to the curious stares and covert whispers his presence had aroused.

For one long moment he held her gaze, and she felt an odd little flutter in the pit of her stomach.

EXAMPLES

- Chief Jepson has just told Rousso that he's been assigned to work with Sally Cooper. And he doesn't like it one bit – because his last female partner got shot. And when he sees Sally he groans – she looks like one puff of wind would blow her away. And those are mean streets out there.

- Or maybe Rousso has been assigned to work with Sean Cooper. They're investigating a string of murders associated with gay nightclubs. And Sean is gay – while Rousso has been hiding his own sexuality since he was a kid. Heck, he even managed to stay married for a while. But Sean is one cool dude, with a grin as wide as Manhattan and shoulders to match.

WHAT TO AVOID

Don't make the initial impression explicitly erotic unless you're writing that kind of book. Your characters' initial reactions to each other should be in keeping with the kind of story you are writing – the kind of things they notice about each other, the kind of reaction they have.

Don't write long and detailed descriptions – tie in the details with thoughts and actions.

RAYNE'S SUGGESTION

"The first impressions don't need to be physical. This depends on who the Point-of-View character's perspective. For example, if she's a brainiac, she may be fascinated by the content of the expert lecturer's speech and not notice his body at all."

ASSIGNMENT

1. Take the scene from your WiP when your lovers first meet, and write it as a screenplay. Keep the stage directions to a minimum – let the dialogue do the talking.

2. (If you prefer, you can try this assignment also with one of the scenarios above, when Rousso meets his new partner.)

3. Fifty years on, your lovers are reminiscing about the first time they met. Write the scene.

CHAPTER 8

FIRST MEETING
IN DISGUISE

Rayne Hall

In this chapter, I'm going to show you a variation that will add interest to the first meeting and build tension for the following chapters.

One of the characters pretends to be someone or something other than he really is. (For simplicity, I'll assume that the person in disguise is male while the other is female, but of course it also works the other way round.)

Perhaps he's an undercover police officer, an investigative reporter, a confidence trickster or an enemy spy who has infiltrated her world in order to harm her, her people, or someone close to her.

He could be practising a casual deception, perhaps to win a bet or to gate-crash a party. Or perhaps she's expecting someone to arrive – the new butler, a messenger from her father, the honoured guest of the banquet – and he doesn't get the chance to correct the impression without embarrassing her and others.

More dramatically, he may be an undercover police officer seeking evidence to arrest her brother, an investigative reporter planning to expose the skeleton in her closet, an enemy infiltrator gaining entry into the stronghold, a confidence trickster after her grandmother's jewels, a secret agent for a foreign nation, or a spy sent by the competition to steal the secret formula.

The scene will sizzle with tension, and lay the groundwork for exciting plot development.

The possibilities are manifold. Here are some ideas to get you started.

VERSION 1: A LIKES AND TRUSTS B, NOT REALISING HE'S AN ENEMY

When B arrives, A is attracted to him. The attraction seems safe – after all, he's her father's friend, the deputy sheriff, the hero who rescued the kidnapped children, a minister of her faith, or some other person worthy of trust. She allows the attraction and opens her heart freely.

B, on the other hand, needs to fight his attraction to A. He can't afford to fall in love.

Perhaps he rejects her advances, because he doesn't want her to get hurt, but of course he can't tell her the reason why. To discourage her affection, he may even act in an unpleasant, rude manner.

Conversely, he may encourage her affections, flirt with her and even seduce her, in order to get access to classified information or the castle stronghold.

A trusting B because of his supposed identity is a potent plot device. It creates enormous tension – not just in this scene, but in the following chapters.

When the two meet again, circumstances may have changed, allowing him to reveal his true identity. However, his lie and breach of trust stand between them. After he deceived her, can she truly trust him now? (Your story may then have a scene in which he confesses. See the chapter 'Time to Confess' for guidance on how to make this exciting.)

Version 1 is great for novels where the relationship is the main plot or a major subplot, and where you want rich emotional drama. Depending on the genre and the plot, the two may eventually get together (they will in a Romance novel), or will forever be kept apart (a heart-wrenching plot device which works especially well in historical fiction).

VERSION 2: A DISLIKES AND MISTRUSTS B, NOT REALISING HE'S AN ALLY

She believes him to be a spy, a dangerous criminal, an enemy infiltrator or other undesirable, so she shuts her heart against him and struggles to suppress the attraction. She doesn't know that he is the hero who has come to rescue her people, or an undercover police officer seeking to bust a drug dealing ring.

In this version, the emotional conflict plays out immediately, as she fights her growing attraction for the unsuitable man. It doesn't have the long-term emotional drama that comes from breach of trust. When he reveals his identity towards the end of the scene or in a later chapter, she will find it relatively easy to forgive the deception.

QUESTIONS TO ASK YOURSELF

- Which of the characters is in disguise, and why?

- What does the disguise involve? (Does the character dress, act, talk differently?)

- Why can't the disguised character reveal his true identity?

- How would A react if she found out B's true identity?

- Who is the Point-of-View character? (From whose perspective does the reader experience the scene?)

- Does the reader know only what the PoV of the scene knows, or is the reader in on the secret?

WHEN THE DISGUISED PERSON IS THE POV

What will happen if he is found out? Raise the stakes, and make the potential consequences as terrible as possible.

How does the disguised character feel about the other? The attraction may be serious or superficial, and this affects his other emotions.

Does he feel embarrassed? Ashamed? Guilty? He may wish he could abandon his mission rather than deceive and harm such a worthy woman.

Does he feel the attraction too? Does he long to open up to her, to enter a relationship? Does he wish he really was the person he pretends to be? Is he tempted, even for a moment, to reveal all? (This temptation may come not in the first meeting scene, but later, when he has come to know and appreciate her.) Of course, he'll remain loyal to his important cause.

On the other hand, he may be delighted that he gets the chance to flirt with (or seduce) the beautiful princess, CEO, or lab technician, and view it as a perk of the job. His main emotions may be triumph, satisfaction or pride. However, to make him likeable, give him some qualms and pangs of conscience in this scene. Of course, later (at the end of the scene or in a future scene) he will regret his deception deeply.

During this scene, arrange it so that he gets almost exposed. Perhaps the woman observes a similarity between him and the long-lost cousin. Maybe he accidentally uses a phrase or mannerism from his native land, lacks a skill the real prince would possess, or reveals knowledge he's not supposed to have. Another character may arrive and recognise him, so he has to brazen it out and persuade that person that she's mistaken. This almost-exposed secret will increase the tension manifold.

WHEN THE DECEIVED PERSON IS THE POV

Her feelings during that first meeting are probably positive, such as hope and relief. She's glad to have found someone she can trust, a suitor of whom her strict father will approve, a man of her own caste and faith. She enjoys being attracted to this man.

However, it's good to give her a moment's doubt somewhere in the scene. Something about this man is not quite right – perhaps a discrepancy in his story – and she questions it. This way, she won't come across as an utter dunce.

BOTH CHARACTERS IN DISGUISE

For most novels, it's best if only one character is in disguise. If both conceal their true identity, the situation can get too complicated for the reader, and the emotional intensity of the experience is reduced.

Both characters in disguise can work well for light-hearted works of fiction (e.g. a Romantic Comedy), especially if the characters assumed the false identity by accident or through a misunderstanding.

To make it work in other genres and serious fiction, at least one character and his motivation need to be already established when the meeting takes place.

READ A SAMPLE

At the end of the book, I've added an excerpt from my novel *Storm Dancer*, a dark epic Fantasy novel.

In the story, the female PoV character Merida has escaped from the harem. Male character Dahoud has the job of hunting her down and returning her to captivity.

Merida assumes the disguise of a whiteseer to avoid being recognised. In this role, she needs to read her pursuer's palms. When that disguise is about to be exposed, she pretends to be a tavern bellydancer. Of course she has to perform, and among the audience is Dahoud. Throughout those scenes, Merida squashes any feelings of attraction rigorously.

I had great fun writing those scenes. Many readers have emailed me to say that those are their favourite chapters in the book. I hope you enjoy reading them.

SUSANNE'S SUGGESTION

"Maybe Character A isn't in disguise, but Character B has made an assumption about who they are – and acts on it. Character A then reacts to that assumption. In my novel *Chasing Stars*, Kat (Character A) is on the yacht owned by Javier (Character B) for reasons of her own – and he catches her hiding in his dressing room:

> *It had happened before – a rather crass attempt to get into his bed, with an eye to a lucrative kiss'n'tell story in the down-market press.*

When he moves in to kiss her, he gets a very unexpected response!"

ASSIGNMENT

Consider the first meeting. Could you add interest by putting one of the characters in disguise? Who would it be, and in what kind of disguise? How does he do it? What does it involve? What would happen if found out? How does the other character react to the supposed identity? Allow yourself some fun as you imagine this scene unfolding.

CHAPTER 9

FALLING IN LOVE – AND INITIAL RESISTANCE

Susanne McCarthy

Falling in love is a delicious part of the story. Make the most of it.

INITIAL RESISTANCE

You will have set up some kind of conflict – a variety of internal and external reasons why this love affair appears to be doomed from the start: she resents him because he was responsible for her father going to prison; he's a warrior, a captain of the Sindril guard, and has no place in his life for a woman.

But then that irresistible attraction – whether or not explicitly sexual – will begin to wreak havoc with those preconceived notions. How is that going to mess with their heads? The first reaction may well be to double-down on their initial prejudices – there's going to be resistance, hostility. You will be able to show this through their dialogue, whether with each other or with other people, as well as through their actions – maybe one or both tries (of course without success) to avoid the other.

They're going to be denying to themselves how they feel – finding other reasons for it, trivialising it, letting off steam in other ways. Of course she feels some attraction to him, on a purely objective level he's very good looking, and besides it's been a long time since she's been in a relationship – she's a little more vulnerable than usual. He takes to the fencing yard, spending hours putting the new batch of guard recruits through a punishing training schedule.

This struggle is getting annoying, affecting their concentration – you can have some fun with scenes showing this: his brother laughs at him when a skinny sixteen-year-old recruit from the southern plains catches him off-guard and nicks the sleeve of his shirt; she spills her tea when she hears his voice behind her. And there will be dreams – jumbled images, half-remembered on waking in sweaty, tumbled sheets.

BUT RESISTANCE IS FUTILE...

Tentatively at first, not quite ready to give up their initial prejudices, they begin to see things in the other which challenges those notions. Maybe small things at first – you can sprinkle these moments into the action: she notices how he seems to take a friendly interest in the well-being of even his most insignificant staff, asking the caretaker about his wife's knee replacement surgery; he realises that even his hard-bitten sword-master has a soft spot for her.

If one of them has a child, that will significantly raise the stakes. There will be a lot of tension, particularly at the first meeting with the child. If this goes badly, it could be a deal breaker. How would you show him interacting with his partner's small daughter? How does she feel, watching them? How will she break the ice with his seven-year-old son? (This could be even more fraught if this is a gay relationship.)

If there isn't a child, maybe there's an animal? Her bonkers but beloved dog? The most nervous horse in the castle stables – or even a crotchety dragon?

Maybe they have to work together on something, which requires them to trust each other. This is going to be difficult – can they *really* trust this person, or are they letting the attraction they can no longer deny overrule their better judgement? They might waver a bit, hesitate before putting everything at risk. If this goes wrong, a lot of things could get broken – including their heart.

MAYBE HE'S NOT SO BAD AFTER ALL...?

People who have been together for many years say the key to a long and happy relationship is simple: you have to like each other. (OK, I lied, it isn't simple at all.) Your readers want to know that these two characters in whose love affair they are investing their time and emotions stand a good chance of being among those who make it for the long haul.

So mere sexual attraction, however hot, is ultimately unsatisfying. You have to give your characters good reasons for falling in love with each other. In a lovely review I got for my novel *Chasing Stars* the reviewer said, "*It was so obvious that Javier needed Kat in his life.*" I punched the air in delight – that was exactly what I was aiming for.

Why do we like people? We find out that they share our core values, we can respect them and feel that they respect us, we feel they are being honest, authentic. We see things in them which reflect the things we like about ourselves (and perhaps the opposite of things we dislike about ourselves.)

We feel they like us, that there is a degree of equality between us – they give us confidence, enhance our self-esteem. They fill a gap in our lives we hadn't even realised was there. And the thing that often seals the deal – that we can have fun together, we can laugh together.

So those are the things you will need to layer into your story, as your characters gradually discover things about each other. As with trust, they may at first feel wary – the initial reasons why they disliked or distrusted this person are still nagging at their minds, whispering warnings, playing on their doubts and insecurities, churning up their emotions.

IT CAN NO LONGER BE DENIED

There will come a moment when the character is forced to admit to themselves that they have fallen in love. This may come as a bit of a shock to them – though the reader was probably miles ahead.

His Kat? Where had that come from?
Life was full of surprises.

WHAT TO AVOID

Don't transition too abruptly from dislike and distrust to falling in love.

RAYNE'S SUGGESTION

"Think back to when you fell in love. What did it feel like? What was the first thing you found attractive about this person? How did you realise you were in love? Try to recall details, and adapt them for your fiction."

FURTHER STUDY

The book *Writing Vivid Emotions* may be a useful next step.

ASSIGNMENTS

1. What characteristic of the love interest does your PoV character like most? When do they realise this? Write a few sentences describing a situation which shows this characteristic.

2. Your PoV character has just come to the realisation that they have fallen in love. What are their thoughts at that moment?

CHAPTER 10

THE COUPLE'S FIRST KISS

Susanne McCarthy

Oh, that first kiss! There are so many things you can do with it. But as in life, it's going to be a pivotal moment – once your lovers have kissed, everything changes. A kiss is an acknowledgement of the sexual spark between them, and once it's been ignited it can never quite be extinguished.

WHEN DOES IT HAPPEN?

- Maybe it happens early on – a mutual flare of chemistry the first time they meet. That's going to mean that things are likely to be pretty hot from then on – particularly if one or both of them reacts with hostility to the kiss

- Maybe they've been building up to it for a while, maybe had a few 'near misses' and *finally* it all just overwhelms them

- Maybe it's a snatched kiss in a moment of tension or danger – maybe catching them both by surprise

- It might be quite tentative, particularly if it's a Young Adult story or a Sweet Romance. Just a meeting of warm lips, the brush of a butterfly's wings

- Maybe he kisses her but she resists, trying to push him away – but then she capitulates. Or maybe she responds at first but then comes to her senses

WHO INITIATES IT?

It would usually be the alpha male – but why not shake it up a little? There's a brilliant scene in *To Have and Have Not*, with Humphrey

Bogart and Lauren Bacall, when she sits on his lap and kisses him. And purrs, "It's even better when you help."

SWEET'N'TENDER OR HOT'N'HARD?

To an extent this will follow from your characters and how they have led up to this, but you don't have to go for the obvious. Your tough-guy hero may kiss like melting honey. It may start sweet'n'tender but quickly become hot'n'hard – or go the other way.

Hot'n'hard: There may not be much preamble to this kind of kiss – it could erupt out of a quarrel or in the middle of a dramatic scene. The language would be quite fierce, almost war-like – capturing, crushing, invading, plundering, yielding. There may be growling, gasping. Your alpha male may be crushing his lover's body close against him so that she is devastatingly aware of his hard male strength.

Sweet'n'tender: You can linger much longer over this kind of kiss, building up to it slowly. How do your lovers look at each other? How do they feel about how the other person is looking at them?

How do they touch? How does it feel? Perhaps he runs his thumb over her trembling lips. As they move together, how does that feel? Often there is a brief moment before the kiss – their breath mingles, or maybe she feels his warm breath on her face. Maybe he kisses her eyes or her temple first.

Then their mouths meet. The language will be all about warmth and softness, coaxing, teasing, melting. A sinuous tongue sliding between soft lips and over sensitive membranes, swirling into deep, secret corners. How is she reacting? Maybe she's curving her supple body against his. Is she feeling a little dizzy, maybe her heart is beating too fast, she's forgotten to breathe? Is she tempted to let it go further, maybe imagining what it would be like?

And what about him? How does it feel having her in his arms? Maybe he's been thinking about it – is it how he imagined? (It's probably better!) He's likely to have kissed a lot of women before – maybe he's startled by how this kiss feels different.

How does the kiss end? Maybe one of them pulls away before it goes too far? Maybe they're interrupted? How does that feel?

From my novel *Christmas Secrets.*

He was stroking his hand down over her hair, and with every breath she was breathing the unique scent of his skin – a subtle, musky maleness that seemed to bypass the rational part of her mind entirely, and reach directly into some primeval core of femininity deep inside her that she had never been aware of.

Slowly she lifted her head, and found herself gazing up into eyes so dark she felt as though she could drown in them. Mesmerising eyes, holding her prisoner as he stroked the tears from her cheeks with his thumb. Her lips parted on a soft indrawn breath as the universe seemed to stand still...

And then slowly, very slowly, he bent his head, and she felt the warm brush of his lips over hers. Something seemed to be melting inside her, and as his arms drew her closer she stretched up on tip-toe, her body curving into the hard length of his as she let herself surrender to the sweet tenderness of his kiss. His languorous tongue swirled over the delicate inner membranes of her mouth in a flagrantly sensual exploration, seeking out all the secret, sensitive corners within, inciting a helpless response.

No-one had ever kissed her like this...

RAYNE'S SUGGESTION

"Kissing means different things to different people. This depends on their cultural and social background, as well as their personal views. For some, kissing is just a bit of light fun with no strings attached, while for others a kiss on the lips practically means they're engaged. What if the two kissers have different expectations about what the kiss will lead to?

The misunderstanding may not become obvious until a later scene, but you'll need to write the kiss so that both characters behave according to their interpretations."

ASSIGNMENT

- Take your lovers' first kiss from your WiP draft and flip it. If he initiates it, have her initiate it. If it's hot'n'hard, make it sweet'n'tender. You may find that the new version is stronger, more moving, and less predictable.

CHAPTER 11

FORMING A RELUCTANT ALLIANCE

Rayne Hall

When two people who hate each other must cooperate for an important cause, the scenes sizzle with tension and romantic potential.

Here are some scenarios in which you can develop the 'reluctant alliance' theme:

- Two police officers who detest each other are assigned a case together because of their complementing skills sets

- The son and daughter of two rival royal houses must marry to end the war and save thousands of lives

- After a bitter divorce, the ex-spouses need each other's help to rescue their child from the clutches of human traffickers

LEARNING TO TRUST

The focus of this type of scene is on trust.

The two characters will probably start distrusting each other intensely, and then, over several scenes, gradually come to trust each other.

In each of those scenes, the enemy-ally character does something trust-inspiring that takes the PoV character by surprise.

Here is an example how one character's attitude gradually changes over several scenes.

"I hate this person! But I'll have to put up with him, for the sake of the important cause."

"I hate him. He's really horrid. But he does have a good side."

"I don't like him. But I can count on him when it really matters."

"He's nice, actually, apart from his [...]"

"Despite everything, he's the person I trust more than anyone else."

"Oh my God, I'm in love with him!"

Each insight surprises both the PoV character and the reader.

The other character's attitude to the relationship changes too, although not as overtly, and not necessarily at the same pace.

Weave this development into other plot events, using the Layering technique. (See the chapter 'Layering Love Scenes with Other Scenes'.)

STARTING THE ALLIANCE

When the two characters agree to the alliance, they may already know each other, or they may meet for the first time. Either way, they dislike each other intensely. Give them several specific, compelling reasons to dislike each other.

Make it clear that despite their dislike, the two characters want the alliance. It's not forced on them. Parents, politicians and superiors may push for the alliance, but the characters have the final choice. If they could opt out but voluntarily go through with it for the sake of the important cause, the reader will root for them.

The moment when they seal their alliance – when they sign the contract, shake hands to seal a promise, say "I do" at the altar – is an important turning point in their relationship and in the book's plot. Flesh it out. Devote several paragraphs to it, showing details.

During this scene, show the reasons for their distaste graphically. Let the readers see why the PoV character hates the enemy ally so much. Reveal that character's arrogance, racism, selfishness in action.

But also show one surprising act of honesty or kindness. Perhaps while they negotiate the contract, he urges adding a clause that will protect her. Or perhaps during the ceremony, she helps a frail old woman who is struggling up the stairs.

WHAT NOT TO DO

Don't leap from total hatred to love in a single scene.

SUSANNE'S SUGGESTION

"For your reader to root for this love to work out, and to accept the characters' change of heart, neither of them can really be evil. Consider basing the hatred on something one character couldn't avoid (perhaps they were just doing their job, for example he prosecuted her father) or a serious misunderstanding (see the chapter on Conflicts).

There are some things which can rarely be reconciled – for example, diametrically opposed political or religious outlooks. Depending on the kind of story you're writing, you may want to avoid those anyway – your readers may also disagree strongly with an extreme point of view."

ASSIGNMENTS

1. Think of the scene in which the two commit to an alliance. What does each hate about the other?

2. Decide which character is the PoV. Now play the scene in your head from that perspective. Graphically show the reasons why

she hates the other person. Show why the cause is so important to her that she commits to the alliance despite her dislike.

3. Think of one small positive thing the enemy-ally does. How can you weave this into the scene?

CHAPTER 12

RACKED BY JEALOUSY

Rayne Hall

Jealousy is a painful feeling – but it can be a useful one, because it alerts a character that another person is threatening the relationship. Forewarned, the jealous person can take action to protect their love.

For fiction writers, creating a jealousy-arousing situation is helpful. It shakes characters out of their complacency, creates emotional tension and keeps readers uncertain about what will happen.

Depending on the plot, the character may or may not have cause for jealousy. The other person may or may not pose a serious threat to the relationship. In a Romance novel, the jealousy is likely to arise from a misunderstanding (she's his stepsister) or from malicious intent – usually by the 'other woman' but sometimes from someone else: His father doesn't want him to marry this little nobody, so tells her he is about to get engages to the beautiful heiress. In other genres, the 'other woman' may destroy the relationship.

EMOTIONS

As well as pure jealousy, the affected character probably feels a whole range of emotions. These may include:

- Suspicion
- Anger
- Worry
- Disappointment
- Jealousy

- Hurt

- Humiliation

When planning the scene, decide which emotions the character feels at what stage.

How do these emotions feel? Where in the body does she feel them?

Describe the physical symptoms of these feelings. This is more effective than stating the emotions.

Instead of

She was suspicious.

Write (for example):

Her stomach knotted.

Or

Her stomach quivered and her heart thumped.

Or

A heavy weight curled in her stomach.

Instead of

She felt jealous.

Write (for example)

Her stomach hardened.

Or:

Her jaw tensed, and spots flashed before her eyes.

Or

Understanding burned a trail of fire in her chest.

HOW TO INSERT JEALOUSY

Let the character observe something that triggers her jealousy. For example, her boyfriend tenderly drapes his jacket across the other girl's shoulder, while she herself is shivering with cold.

After showing the trigger, describe her visceral response. Only then does she respond overtly.

The overt response may or may not admit how she feels.

For example:

> *Mary shivered and hugged herself, wishing she brought a cardigan.*
>
> *She glanced at John who was standing chatting to someone in the gazebo, and gave him a quick wave to signal that she wanted to go home. But he didn't catch her glance. Instead, she heard him laugh. Now she saw his companion's face: it was the French girl again.*
>
> *John was draping his leather jacket across the girl's shoulders.*
>
> *Mary's stomach hardened. With an unconcerned smile plastered to her face, she marched to the gazebo.*

For best effect, weave the jealousy as a subplot into another scene, in which the character must deal with important matters. Perhaps she is even forced to hide her emotions and act as if everything was fine.

The jealousy may develop slowly, perhaps over several scenes, beginning as a mild niggle and growing into raging agony.

WHAT TO AVOID

Don't state the emotion outright. (*She was jealous.*) It's more compelling as well as more realistic if the PoV character isn't aware of her own jealousy. Describe her visceral reactions (the physical symptoms) instead.

SUSANNE'S TIP

"As with conflicts, it is important that there are good enough reasons for the jealousy. This may arise from the current situation, or it may be that the current situation is a painful echo of something that happened in the past – perhaps she found her ex-fiancé in bed with her best friend, or his ex-wife ran off with his business rival."

FURTHER STUDY

You may find my book *Writing Vivid Emotions* useful in this context.

ASSIGNMENT

Identify a situation in your novel where the PoV character feels jealous. What exactly triggers the jealousy? Choose a specific detail and write a sentence or paragraph about it.

Now write a sentence describing the character's visceral response. Follow this with a sentence or paragraph that shows what she does to deal with the situation or to hide her feelings.

CHAPTER 13

TIME TO CONFESS

Rayne Hall

When one lover makes a confession, the emotional stakes are high. How will the other react? How does this affect the relationship?

The scene is a turning point in the relationship, and it is potentially one of the most emotionally tense scenes in the novel.

My suggestions apply to any gender, although for readability I'll assume that the confessing character is male, and the recipient of the confession female.

WHAT TO CONFESS?

He must tell her the truth about something that he has hidden or lied about until now. Here are some examples:

- He had an affair with his assistant
- He isn't the manager of the factory as he had claimed, but a foreman worker
- He is already married
- He is betrothed to someone else
- He isn't the person he pretended to be
- He has an illegitimate child (fathered before their marriage – or during)
- He isn't as wealthy as he claimed
- He has gambled away their fortune

- He has sold her as a slave. (In some historical societies, a husband had the right to sell his wife.)

- He has a sexually transmitted disease

- He is in love with her sister

- It was he who killed her beloved pet dog

- Her miscarriage wasn't an accident, but arranged by him

- It was he who stole the jewels – a crime for which her brother was hanged

- He is gay

These are of course extreme examples. Other confessions may be relatively minor, but those won't require a full scene for themselves. You can incorporate minor confessions into another scene, using the same techniques but toning them down.

WHY IS THIS CONFESSION SO DIFFICULT?

Make it as difficult as possible for him to tell her the truth. He knows that the truth will hurt her, that it will change their relationship, that it will destroy her trust in him, that he may lose her love, or that she may leave him.

That's why he kept the truth from her for so long.

Why is it this truth so devastating for her? Create several reasons, and make them as intense as possible, so the truth is unbearable.

Let's take one example: Her miscarriage wasn't an accident, but arranged by him. That is shocking and devastating enough – but you can make it worse.

- What if as the result of the miscarriage, she can never become pregnant again?

- What if this was her only chance of ever having a child?

- What if her childlessness makes her an outcast in a society where a woman's worth depends on motherhood?

- What if she had loved that unborn child like she had never loved anything or anyone?

- What if that child, if born, would have secured the succession to the throne and prevented the devastating war that cost thousands of lives?

- What if he is the figurehead of an anti-abortion campaign, and must now reveal himself as a hypocrite?

- What if he swore an oath – perhaps on his wife's life – that it was an accident, and now he must admit that the oath was false?

- What if an innocent person got punished for causing the miscarriage?

Pile it on, make it as awful as you can.

WHY IS HE TELLING IT NOW?

He hid the truth for a long time. The longer he kept the secret, the more difficult it became to confess. So why does he confess now? There must be a reason for the timing. Here are some ideas:

- Someone else is going to tell her, and he wants her to hear the truth from him, not anyone else

- He is getting blackmailed

- They're about to enter a new stage in their relationship – for example, they're getting married – and he wants her to know the truth before she commits

- He fears that she is about to discover the truth

- He is suspected of a horrible crime that carries the death penalty, the only way to prove his innocence is to provide an alibi for that night – which requires him to come clean about where and with whom he had spent the night

HOW DOES HE TALK?

Be aware of his emotions. What does he feel? What does he expect will happen? What outcome does he hope for? What outcome does he fear? How does he rally the courage to finally speak the truth?

In this type of scene, body language (posture, movement, gestures, facial expressions, tone of voice, visceral responses) creates reader emotion.

Describe the character's voice as he confesses – does he stutter, speak in a low voice, or talk fast to get it over with?

How does he stand or sit? How does he move? Does he look at her while he confesses, or at the floor? What does he do with his hands?

To get his approach, voice and body language right, consider what he feels. He probably feels several different emotions during the scene such as nervousness, fear, determination, guilt, embarrassment, shame, regret and remorse.

HOW DOES SHE REACT?

On hearing the truth, she will be shocked and shaken. She will struggle to process the information, and need time to assess and decide.

During this scene, she will experience a vast range of intense emotions. These may include: apprehension, dread, confusion, shock, disgust, hatred, hurt, insecurity, disbelief, fear, jealousy, fury, resentment, hopelessness, resignation, depression, sadness, grief, unhappiness, despair.

If you write the scene from the confession recipient's PoV, let the reader feel her visceral reactions. If the scene is in the confessing character's PoV, show the other person's body language.

Her reaction will come in stages, as she processes what he has told her. Her first response probably doesn't reflect her final assessment and decision. Indeed, she may need several days to absorb the enormity of what happened, and to come to terms with it one way or another.

HOW TO END THIS SCENE

A good way to close this scene is with confession-receiver sending the confession-giver away. This is realistic. It can express her anger ("Get out of my sight!"), confusion ("Please go. I need to be alone.") or any other emotion. It also keeps the emotional tension high.

If you use the 'scene & sequel' method of scene structuring, this ending will fit neatly into a 'sequel' section in which the PoV character reflects, processes and plans.

HOW DOES THE RELATIONSHIP CHANGE?

The relationship between the two will never be the same again.

Now the confessing character's true role or identity is revealed, it affects who he is and how she treats him.

Even more importantly, he has broken her trust by lying to her continuously. She won't be able to trust him again completely, not for a long time. From now on, she will be wary of anything he says, claims or promises.

The relationship changes the moment the truth is out. It will continue to change over the next scenes, as both characters come to terms with what happened, and learn to trust again. It is possible that for the next days, weeks or months he is on 'probation' before she decides whether or not to forgive him.

In the long term, the relationship may become stronger, because it is now based on honesty, and because there is now genuine understanding between them.

But the relationship may not survive. When she finds out the terrible thing he's done, and realises how he has deceived her and that everything between them was based on a lie, she may break it off. However much she loves him, she will sooner or later come to realise that the person she loved existed only in her wishful imagination, and that this man does not deserve her trust.

If the deception leads to the end of the relationship, you can find tips in the chapter 'Breaking Up'.

WHAT NOT TO DO

The recipient of the confession shouldn't immediately forgive. That would be unrealistic, and it would miss a great opportunity for emotional drama.

SUSANNE'S SUGGESTION

"The impact of the scene will vary with how you place it in your story. How much has she been lured into trusting him? Have they made love, even got married? Has she lent him money?

Has she had suspicions but has told herself she was wrong? Has he brushed her doubts aside, accused her of imagining things? 'Gaslighting' is a classic technique of psychological manipulation, where the manipulator causes the victim to doubt her own perception of reality. You can Google it to learn more."

ASSIGNMENTS

1. Why did the character in our story harbour this secret for so long? Why is it such a terrible thing to confess? Why does he choose this moment to confess? What emotions does he feel in

this scene? Select several visible body language clues or visceral responses to convey these emotions.

2. Why is this revelation so devastating for the character who receives the confession? What hope and beliefs does this shatter in her? What emotions does she feel in this scene? Select several visible body language clues or visceral responses to convey these emotions.

3. How does the scene end?

CHAPTER 14

FINAL COMMITMENT – AND PERHAPS A PROPOSAL OF MARRIAGE

Susanne McCarthy

At some point, usually towards the end of your story, the physical attraction and the rational realisation of liking and trust meld together to overcome the barriers, and your characters will finally acknowledge that they are falling in love – acknowledge it to themselves at least.

Because the last act of the story is when they take the risk of sharing their innermost thoughts and feelings, their doubts and fears. This is when the misunderstandings and conflicts which have come between them are exposed, and finally resolved. This needs to be carefully controlled – not just a back-and-forth, but following an arc:

- Grievances are exposed – maybe on each side, maybe more come out as the conversation goes on. This stage may become quite heated.

- As the quarrel begins to reach a crisis point, they each realise that if they do not state the truth about what they are thinking and feeling, the relationship cannot survive. Finally they will say the things they were afraid to say before – the assumptions they had made about the other person, things about themselves they have been hiding

- The other reacts – with surprise, shock, sadness. But now it's all out in the open, they can begin to understand each other, assure each other that those things which seemed so dangerous really don't matter at all, forgive each other

And then at last they can say the "I love you." What are they thinking? Who speaks first? What do they say? How do they say it – do they blurt it out, or murmur it in the middle of a kiss? Maybe they admit that they have loved from the beginning, or that it's something that they came to realise at a particular moment: "*It was when you rescued that kitten from the tree. I knew right then I was in love with you.*"

How will the other person respond? Hesitantly, happily? This is a moment to linger over. Maybe they will begin to voice their hopes for the future – which will usually include marriage.

MARRIAGE PROPOSAL

The conclusion to most love stories, or stories with a strong love interest, is likely to be a marriage proposal. Not necessarily, of course – you could leave it with the clear indication that your couple have made a serious, long-term commitment without necessarily mentioning marriage. But most readers probably want the flowers-and-confetti thing.

It may also be that they are already married – maybe one of those 'coerced marriage' stories. But at the end, when all the conflicts and misunderstandings have been cleared up, they agree to make their marriage a real one.

WHO POPS THE QUESTION?

In most heterosexual relationships it would be the man. Yes, in real life it sometimes happens the other way round, but if you're going to shake up traditional expectations like that you'd better make it good. You might use a touch of humour here, but you need to make it very clear that he's absolutely delighted by the idea. Or maybe he's previously proposed – once or several times – but she's turned him down. Now, with everything sorted, she raises the subject. "You know what you said yesterday…?" "If the offer's still open…?"

In gay or lesbian couples, either one can take the lead, although it will probably be obvious from the way you have written the characters and the relationship which one it is most likely to be. Though again, shake it up if you want to. In historical novels, and in contemporary novels set in many countries, the couple would be debarred from taking the legal step, but they may arrange their own ceremony, either in private or with family and friends.

THE BIG MOMENT

Has he planned the scene in advance? A romantic dinner for two, a boat-ride through Paris? I'll bet you a dime to a dollar that if he has, it's going to go wrong! The flambé catches fire and they have to evacuate the restaurant, both soaked by the sprinklers in the ceiling. They get mugged as they're about to board the boat, and he beats up the assailant and then gets arrested and they end up in a chilly *gendarmerie* station waiting for the inspector to confirm that there will be no charges.

Or maybe, although he has been thinking about it, the actual moment arises out of the immediate action. And he may not actually say, "Will you marry me?" For example, in my novel *Practiced Deceiver,* Ross and Alysa have just come out of court, where Alysa's mother was on a driving charge:

> "All right. But the Registry Office is in the next building to this one. We're going over there right now to sort out a special licence. And then you can ring Alain and ask him to send that dress over on the next plane. I intend to make this relationship legal and binding before you can change your mind."

SHE SAID YES!

Think about how she will respond. Will she be surprised, will she still have a little doubt as to whether he really means it? Then she will realise that the dream really has come true – what emotions will she be feeling at this point, what will she say and how will she say it? There may be tears, there will certainly be tenderness. There may be kisses, they may make love again – though it's rather nice to let them go off on their own this time.

This is from my novel *No Place for Love*:

> *"I think I must have sensed I was waiting for something else all along."*
>
> *"'Waiting for what?" she asked, her voice a little unsteady as she risked a look into those deep, dark, hypnotic eyes.*
>
> *"Something very precious," he murmured, his voice taking on a husky timbre as he stopped walking and drew her into his arms. "A woman who knows what love really is, who could show me what it means to care."*
>
> *His lips brushed over hers, light as a butterfly's wings, and she felt herself melting, all her dreams flowing together into this one sweet moment. She lifted her arms to wrap them tightly around his neck, kissing him back with all the vibrant love in her heart.*
>
> *He lifted his head, his dark eyes gazing down into hers. "I think I'm going to have to become a perpetual student of the subject," he murmured teasingly. "In which case, there's only one thing to do – I shall have to marry the teacher."*
>
> *Lacey's violet-blue eyes widened in astonishment, but she knew from the tenderness in his smile that he meant it. "I... Yes!" she breathed, her heart spilling over. "Oh, yes please!"*

WHAT TO AVOID

Don't rush it – readers of romance novels love to linger over this part of the story. You may throw in an epilogue – the wedding, the birth of their first (or fifth) child.

RAYNE'S SUGGESTION

"When one partner proposes, the other is expected to make a decision that affects the rest of her life. Is she prepared for this? Has she considered in advance how she'll respond if he pops the question? If yes, has she been hoping or anticipating the question? For how long?

But perhaps she didn't expect a proposal. Will she be carried away by the romance of the moment and agree spontaneously, or will she be sensible and ask for time to consider, even though her heart has already said yes?

What if one of the lovers is ready to make the final commitment, but the other not quite? Will the 'ready' partner try to persuade the other to commit, or encourage her to think it through?

Perhaps the final commitment occurs in two stages over two different scenes, with only one partner committed at first, and the other later.

These aspects need to be aligned with the lovers' personalities, their relationship, and their past experiences of love.

Also consider that 'marriage' is not the only way a couple can commit to each other. Perhaps in the context of your story, the final commitment means something different, but it should still be significant for the lovers as well as for your readers."

ASSIGNMENTS

1. Focus on the moment when your PoV character is going to say, "I love you." What are they thinking, what will they say, how will they say it?

2. Draft your proposal scene from your WiP – but place your couple in the most awkward situation you can think of. And/ or write it with the opposite person making the proposal.

CHAPTER 15

BREAKING UP

Rayne Hall

When lovers break up, they feel intense emotions – whether it's anger or regret, relief or pain. Know what your characters feel, and let the reader feel the same.

If you deal with the break-up in just a few short lines, it won't convince the reader. A reader who sees nothing more than this two-line exchange "This is unforgivable. I don't ever want to see you again." "As you wish. It's over between us." will expect the couple to calm down and reconcile.

In this chapter, we're looking at genuine break-ups. (In Romance, final break-ups are rare, but they can be a crucial part of the plot in other genres.)

They deserve a lot more space, probably a whole scene, although the scene may be layered with other plot elements. (See the Chapter 'Layering Love Scenes With Other Scenes'.)

Genuine break-ups don't happen on the spur of the moment. At least one of the lovers has thought the matter through. The second character may have seen it coming, or may be taken by surprise.

Even if they part by mutual consent, one of them takes the initiative, while the other reacts. In this chapter, I'll call them the 'upbreaker' and the 'upbreakee' – words I've invented just now.

- Who initiates the break-up, and why?

- How does the other feel about it?

- Why does the upbreaker choose this particular moment to announce the decision?

- Does he try to break it to her gently, so as to hurt her as little as possible, or does he want her to suffer?

CONFLICTED FEELINGS

Although the upbreaker knows that she's doing the right thing, and really wants the affair to end, part of her still clings to the relationship. She hopes against hope that things will change in the last minute, and that the break-up can be averted.

This is especially true if they have been together for a long time, if they have planned a future together, or if she loves him intensely.

Example: After eight years as John's mistress, Mary finally realises that he will never leave his wife for her, despite his repeated promises. She wants to end the relationship and make a fresh start. When she tells him it's over, part of her hopes that he'll say, "My wife has agreed to the divorce. We went to see a solicitor this morning. Look, here are the signed documents." Of course she knows this won't happen, but the hope is there.

REFUSING TO ACCEPT

The upbreakee won't simply say "yes, okay" at once, but will react with an emotion – surprise, shock, hurt, humiliation, disbelief – before responding. You can show this emotion with a visceral reaction or with body language.

Then he'll either accept it, or fight for the relationship.

If he accepts, show that it is with a heavy heart, or at least that he is in two minds about it. Write something like this:

> *He sat staring at his hands for a long time, motionless. Then he faced her. "If this is what you truly want, I won't stand in your way."*

More likely, the upbreakee will fight to preserve the relationship, putting forward reasons why they must stay together, and pleading with the upbreaker to give him and their love another chance.

Example: Mary discovered that her boyfriend John has been cheating on her – again. She no longer trusts him and tells him it's over. John pleads with her to give him another chance, promises that this time he'll really stay faithful.

Add a few lines in which the upbreakee pleads for another chance. Together with the upbreaker's own conflicted emotions, this can clench the reader's heart.

EMOTIONS AND BODY LANGUAGE

During a break-up, both characters run through a gamut of emotions.

For a PoV character, you can spell out the emotions, perhaps by showing how it feels physically (visceral responses). For the non-PoV, use facial expression and posture. For both, you can use tone of voice.

Decide on at least three emotions for each character. I recommend five or more.

Here are some suggestions to choose from, although you may add others: regret, resentment, hurt, relief, fear, guilt, embarrassment, shame, anger, triumph, hatred, longing, despair, pity, hope, humiliation, triumph.

Some emotions will be present throughout the scene, others will come and go.

For example, a character may feel guilt, then pity, then relief. Or he may feel anger at first, then confusion and disbelief, and finally humiliation and hurt.

The characters may not admit those emotions openly, but may try to hide or suppress them.

AFTER THE BREAK-UP

If you use the 'scene & sequel' format of scene structure, the sequel should be filled with the PoV character's emotions, showing how she feels after the break-up. Instead of spelling them out, describe them viscerally: *Hollow pain ached in her chest where love and hope used to be.*

She may tell herself that she's done the right thing, that it's wonderful to be free, that she can now make a new start. Or she may plot how to get the man back.

WHAT NOT TO DO

Don't deal with the break-up in a few quick lines, and don't skimp on emotions.

SUSANNE'S SUGGESTION

"An odd thing about loss – whether through a break-up or a bereavement – is that it's often the small details that trigger the strongest grief. Finding the scarf she left behind, almost laying his place for dinner, realizing that the dog misses him too.

And of course, scents – somehow they go straight past all our consciousness and hit the memory buttons in our brains: scents on the bed-sheets or an old shirt, someone walking past wearing the perfume she used to wear."

FURTHER STUDY

Consider the book *Writing Vivid Emotions* in the Writer's Craft series. It shows in detail how to convey emotions through body language and visceral responses.

ASSIGNMENTS

1. Who initiates the break-up, why, when and how?

2. Decide on several emotions for each character. For each emotion, find a way to convey it without spelling it out – either with a visceral response (for the PoV character) or a body language clue (for the non-PoV).

CHAPTER 16

SACRIFICES FOR LOVE

Rayne Hall

A love scene involving a sacrifice can be an emotionally intense experience for your readers. If you handle it right, they'll choke, cry, and remember this scene (and therefore your book) for the rest of their lives.

THREE SACRIFICE SCENARIOS

The character gives up something that's tremendously important to her in order to make the relationship work. Or she sacrifices the relationship for a greater cause. Or, most heart-wrenching, she sacrifices the relationship out of love.

Let's look at these three options. See if one of them could work in your story.

1. Sacrifice **for** the relationship

She gives up her home, her career, her ambition, her family, her culture, her ideals, her religion, her alliance, her friends or her dreams in order to be with him. This works well in Romance novels where love always wins and is always worth the sacrifice. Make the sacrifice significant. Don't devalue it by revealing afterwards that the career she gave up would have come to an end anyway.

The partner must understand how great the sacrifice is, and appreciate it. Ideally, he too sacrifices something to be with her.

2. Sacrifice **of** the relationship

The two love each other greatly, and yearn to be together... but something else is even more important, so they sacrifice their love for the greater cause. This is a powerful plot situation especially in Historical Fiction and Epic Fantasy. For example, the queen must marry someone else in order to bring an end to the war and save the lives of her subjects. To make this scene utterly heart-wrenching, let the two lovers agree that the sacrifice is necessary. Their unity in this painful decision shows that they are true soulmates.

3. Sacrifice of the relationship for **love**

This type is rare, but is the most heart-wrenching of them all. The character loves the other person so much that he sets her free. For example, she has a spiritual calling to become a celibate nun. Although they're engaged to be married and he loves her deeply, he understands that she will never be happy unless she follows her religious vocation. So he releases her from the betrothal. Or perhaps she's married to someone else, and will lose her child if she gets divorced. Knowing that her child means more to her than anything else, and that the child depends on its mother, he relinquishes his claim on her.

HOW TO HANDLE THE DILEMMA

Make the sacrifice significant. The bigger the sacrifice, the more meaningful it is, and the more memorable the scene becomes.

The character who brings the sacrifice has already thought about it before the scene. She may have made her decision beforehand, or she may arrive at her decision only now, but either way, she knows exactly what she's doing. This isn't a spur-of-the-moment act.

The reader must understand her reasons. Your reader may regret her choice, but must understand it.

Later in the book, you can reveal whether or not she has made the right decision. (In Romance, when she brings the sacrifice for the relationship, it's a given that she's made the right choice, because her lover is worth it.)

Her lover should appreciate the sacrifice. In real life, some people take it for granted that others bring sacrifices – but if that happened in a story, it wouldn't be a love scene.

WHAT NOT TO DO

Don't make the sacrifice a spur-of-the moment decision.

Don't devalue the enormity of the sacrifice by revealing that what she gave up was not worth keeping anyway.

SUSANNE'S SUGGESTION

"In all the core Romantic subgenres, a Happy-Ever-After is expected. If the reader doesn't get it, they're likely to feel cheated. And most of the main romance publishers wouldn't be interested. So Scenarios 2 and 3 wouldn't work as the climax of your story.

However, you could have the sacrifice occurring earlier – and then perhaps becoming the root of a misunderstanding. Maybe he leaves her because he knows she wants children but he can't have them, maybe she leaves him because his father will disinherit him if he marries her. They keep the sacrifice a secret, because they believe that if the other person knows, *they* may make a sacrifice to keep the relationship, which they would come to resent later.

This will lead to scenes of painful internal conflict, pushing the loved one away. The loved one will be confused, maybe angry, may take a while to accept the false excuses.

And then, of course, you would have the later scenes of reconciliation, leading to... the Happy-Ever-After."

ASSIGNMENT

Is there a moment in your novel where you could develop a sacrifice love scene? Which of the three types applies?

Think about how you can show that the other partner truly understands.

CHAPTER 17

GAY LOVE SCENES

Rayne Hall

When writing about love between two people of the same gender, all the same criteria apply as for 'straight' love scenes. Love is love, and a love scene is a love scene.

However, there are some extra factors to take into account.

SETTING

When gay people date, they may choose to meet out of the public eye, or in another town where they are not recognised, especially if one or both of them is not 'out'.

In a public place they may modify their behaviour, e.g. avoid displays of affection. A straight couple can hug or hold hands, but gays may choose to exercise restraint, so as not to provoke hostilities from the homophobic people around them.

INITIAL FLIRTATION

The beginning of a relationship may be slower and more cautious, as they probe each other's orientation. Small gestures that indicate romantic or erotic interest from a person of the opposite sex don't necessarily mean the same thing between people of the same gender.

For example, if a woman receives a male neighbour in her home wearing only sparse clothing, it usually signals that she's open to physical advances. But if a man receives his male neighbour the same way, it may mean nothing other than that he's in a relaxed mood.

If a woman hugs an unhappy male friend and strokes his head, murmuring soothing words, it's a clue that she is ready to take their relationship beyond platonic friendship. But if she does the same with a female friend, it may be the simple act of a close friend.

So unless they can both be certain that the other person is also gay – perhaps because they met in a gay bar – the first love scene will probably involve small cautious steps.

Gay author Yorgos KC advises: "Usually there is a need of much friendly type of interaction between the gay character and the not-known-if-gay character until the moment when he'll be feeling either safe enough to try to go a little further, or too much in love to not do the step. So, the approach should be extra careful and polite."

COMMITMENT

Committing to a relationship, showing the world their love, introducing a person of the same sex as your partner, often involves great sacrifices from one or both.

Unless they are fully 'out', unless they live in a tolerant society, and unless all their family and friends support their homosexual identity, committing to a gay relationship can cost them their friendships, their jobs, their status in society, even their lives.

If a character needs to prepare his children for the revelation, this will delay the commitment. If he has to choose between his parents and his lover, it will make the commitment bittersweet. Use this inner and outer conflict to add emotional richness to that scene.

Study especially the chapters 'Inner, Outer and Relationship Conflicts', 'Final Commitment – And Perhaps a Proposal of Marriage' and 'Sacrifice for Love'.

THE PHYSICAL SIDE

Many straight authors believe that all gay love scenes involve sex. However, you can write your love scene as chaste or as steamy as the plot, the characters and your personal taste require.

When writing about sex between two women or two men, many writers assume that the act always mirrors penetrative sex between heterosexuals, so they obsess about strap-on dildos and such. But sex between two people of the same gender often plays out without any form of penetration.

What if you want to write graphically about sex between two men? Again, I'm handing this over to gay author Yorgos KC, who has this advice:

"Two guys cannot have penetrative sex without some preparation, for natural reasons. Unless of course they don't care about staying clean. So, if something unexpected happens, either they should have cleaned themselves in advance for some unconnected reason, or they should not go for a full course. It is nice to write it, and let the characters' lust lead the way, but it is unrealistic and for any gay guy reading it, it will sound wrong.

Also, a very common mistake I've seen: You can't have a virgin guy receiving a dick with easiness, or feeling a little pain in the beginning, but then everything is pleasant. This is unrealistic. The other guy should prepare him before the penetration. Licking, fingering, lubricating him somehow (KY is the most well-known lubricant and it is a pharmaceutical product – not the best, but the most commonly known). After the anus has relaxed, then yes, it will be pleasant and yes, the virgin guy will feel a little pain in the beginning even after a good preparation, but this pain will give place to pleasure fast enough. Even more if the guy is so much in love, or so horny, that he doesn't care about it."

SUSANNE'S SUGGESTION

"Avoid clichés like the plague. We are just beginning to escape from the binary male/female model of sexuality, but there is still a tendency to impose it on same-gender relationships. We are beginning at last to understand that gender identity can be fluid – individuals may be bisexual, transvestite, transgender, gender-neutral or anything that they feel matches their inner self. That gives you considerable scope to play with!"

ASSIGNMENTS

1. Consider the environment in which the relationship and the love scene play out. What is the general attitude of the population towards gays? How does this affect the couple's behaviour?

2. How open or how secretive are the lovers about their orientation? Are they at the same stage of openness, or is one still 'in the closet', or does one prefer to keep his orientation private? In what ways do their different attitudes complicate the relationship? How do the attitudes of friends and family members affect their relationship?

3. Based on your answers in #1 and #2, consider how these factors can come into play during the love scene. Try to think of several ideas.

CHAPTER 18

DIFFERENT CULTURES, DIFFERENT SPECIES

Rayne Hall

In this chapter, we'll look at love scenes between people of different cultures. 'Culture' in this context can have many meanings. Perhaps one comes from Denmark and the other from Nigeria. Perhaps one is from the present and the other has time-travelled from Ancient Rome. Maybe one hails from a rural farming community while the other is a city person, or one is an indentured serf while the other is a rich aristocrat.

CULTURAL BACKGROUNDS

When the two characters come from different backgrounds, the different customs, expectations, social roles, religions and values affect their relationship greatly. You may want to spend extra time researching those cultures, to make sure you get the differences right.

Every scene between the two – especially the love scenes – reflects a learning process as they come to understand the other better, adapt and compromise.

Don't treat the differences lightly. Make them part of the conflicts in the scene. (See the chapter 'Inner, Outer and Relationship Conflicts'.

Also consider the influence and expectations of the society they come from, because this will affect how they approach the relationship and how they show (or don't show) their feelings. When people come from different cultures, their communities may strongly disapprove. Commitment to the lover may require characters to sever ties with their families – a huge sacrifice. Consult the chapters 'Final Commitment – And Perhaps a Proposal of Marriage' and 'Sacrifice for Love'.

SOME POINTS TO CONSIDER

- How do the courting customs differ between the cultures? (For example, in one culture a kiss is a bit of casual fun without great meaning, whereas in the other culture it signifies betrothal.)

- How do gender roles differ? (For example, in one society females are considered subservient, in the other they are equal.)

- How do people in each culture view those of the other culture? (Perhaps they see the other culture as inferior or an evil influence – or perhaps they view it as superior, possessed of riches or spiritual salvation.)

- Do the two cultures have different religions? If yes, in what areas do those religions clash?

- What misunderstandings may arise from their different habits and traditions?

ETHNICITY

Belonging to different ethnic groups doesn't necessarily create cultural conflicts. For example, take two New-York-bred Protestant stockbrokers in New York, one black and one white – their skin colour differs, but their cultural background is the same. (On the other hand, if one of them falls in love with a tribal shaman in Ghana, culture clash is inevitable.)

However, where cultures conflict, the race issue is likely to emphasise and intensify the problems, perhaps in the form of parental disapproval and religious taboos.

LANGUAGE

If the two characters stem from different cultures, they probably speak different languages. How do they communicate? What misunderstandings arise?

Consider showing one character's progress with the other's language in the love scene. It signifies serious interest and willingness to learn and adapt, and can be a sign of true love.

SPECIES

If you're writing Fantasy, Science Fiction or Paranormal Romance, the two lovers may belong to different species. One may be human, the other could be an extra-terrestrial, a werewolf, a mermaid or a vampire.

The same factors apply as for cultures, but the problems will be more extreme. Don't gloss over them – use them to add tension and conflict to the scene.

One other factor to consider is how the lovers can consummate their relationship. Even you are not showing graphic sex, even if the couple stay chaste throughout the novel, you need to know – because your readers are curious.

When reading about a romance between a human and a member of another species, the reader's curiosity is piqued: Does the mermaid have genitals? Can the bloodless vampire get an erection?

You need to provide the answer, either in the love scene or in a different context. Otherwise the reader will obsess about it and the story will lack plausibility.

WHAT TO AVOID

Don't treat the differences lightly or gloss over them. Instead, make them an important feature in the plot.

SUSANNE'S SUGGESTION

Unfortunately in most modern societies, racism – particularly skin colour – is an unavoidable issue. It can create difficulties for the most loving couples. Will the white partner be able to fully understand how racism has affected the other's life, their perceptions, their anxieties? Will the black partner take longer to trust? And what about the reactions of their families and friends?

ASSIGNMENT

1. Make a list of cultural differences, both large and small, which may affect the couple's relationship.

2. Choose one or several of them to use in the plot of the scene.

CHAPTER 19

WHEN SEVERAL CHARACTERS ARE INVOLVED

Rayne Hall

In this chapter, I'm going to show you techniques you can apply to very different plot scenarios:

- Several lovers (e.g. polygamous, polyandrous, polyamorous and *ménage* relationships)

- One pair of lovers and another character who is involved in the relationship in a non-romantic non-erotic way (for example, a single mum, her son and the prospective husband-stepdad)

TENSIONS

Multiple characters in a love scene means multiple tensions – the same kind of jealousies, insecurities, resentments, dominance issues and conflicts that beset a one-to-one relationship. The tension between any two of them affects all relationships within the unit. The love scenes reflect that, at least in the subtext.

Examples:

If one woman in a polygamous marriage suffers from painful jealousy, her husband and her fellow wife will be aware of her torment when they are enjoying intimate time together.

A single mum whose son violently opposes his prospective stepdad will find the romantic date a bittersweet experience.

STRUCTURE

For a scene that is dialogue-rich and involves conscious decision-making (such as a first kiss, a break-up, a final commitment) you may want to put the focus of the scene on two characters, with the other partner appearing at the beginning or the end of the scene.

Example: The scene begins with A and B together. C enters and is welcomed. B withdraws with a loving smile, leaving A and C alone in the room.

Alternatively, try the following approach which can involve all characters equally.

SHOWING THE UNIT

To show how harmoniously the three (or more) partners function as a unit, show them working together to deal with a major danger or calamity.

Perhaps they cooperate to put out a wildfire or to rescue a child from quicksand.

This type of scene needs little dialogue. Indeed, the fact that they work together so effectively without using many words emphasises what a good unit they are.

The best place for such a scene is shortly after the unit threatened to fall apart because of tensions and resentments. The reader sees how these resentments drop away when something more important is at stake.

Consider using such a scene at the climax of your novel.

PRONOUNS

Whenever a scene involves more than two characters, it can be difficult for the reader to keep up with who the pronouns 'he, his, him' (or 'she, her') refer to. You may need to use names more often than you normally would, or think of other useful clues.

SUSANNE'S SUGGESTION

"If you are writing about a polygamous relationship, how your characters react and relate to each other will reflect the cultural context – whether Earth-bound or fantasy. Is it the expected – even legal – norm? If so, she may feel guilty about feeling jealous, possessive. In scenes where they are all together, she may try to hide these feelings, perhaps try to be extra-loving to her fellow-wife."

ASSIGNMENTS

1. Write a brief section (30-120 words) in which one character withdraws to leave the other two alone together. Write it so that it implies that character's approval.

2. What kind of emergency or calamity might occur that brings those characters to work together as a team?

CHAPTER 20

BUILDING EROTIC TENSION

Susanne McCarthy

From the moment your two lovers meet you will start to build the erotic tension between them. How quickly this progresses depends on the kind of story you are writing: in mainstream romantic fiction and where the romance is part of another genre it may build slowly through most of the story, while in an erotic romance it would be quite rapid – but it's still nice to linger a little over that delicious fizz of initial attraction.

During this time the tension will be building while the plot is going on around them – in most stories you will engineer your plot to bring them together frequently, either alone or with other people around. She will be watching him during a boardroom presentation, fascinated by the way his strong hands toy with his pencil; he will be distracted from his workout in the gym by the gazelle-like creature running on the treadmill beside him.

And now and then their eyes will meet – maybe she'll look away quickly, hoping he won't notice the blush in her cheeks. Or there will be moments when they touch – they shake hands at the end of the board meeting, he offers his hand as she steps down from the carriage.

Those moments will ignite a visceral reaction – her heart may thud, her mouth feel suddenly dry, he may snap the pencil he is holding. As the tension builds, those reactions may become more… well, erotic. Her breasts may ache, her nipples may tingle, he may feel a tightening in his gut and be glad he's sitting down to conceal the evidence of his interest.

Thereafter the steps of the dance can become quite complex, weaving its way through your plot or creating the plot itself. You can build the erotic tension through having your PoV character fantasise:

In my novel *Christmas Secrets:*

> *Another shimmer of heat ran through her body, and she darted a nervous glance across at the door, remembering a little belatedly that she had forgotten to lock it. He could just walk straight in – and she was lying here, naked, the soft water lapping at the creamy curves of her breasts. What if he should come up the stairs? What would he do? What would she do…?*
>
> *She closed her eyes again, her fevered imagination painting the scene… The door opening slowly, him crossing the room towards her, his gaze hot and hungry as he looked down at her. And then he would scoop her up out of the bath as easily as he had scooped her out of the snow, carry her off to his bedroom and lay her down on that spectacular bed, among the satin sheets…*

Then the powerful physical attraction between them begins to overcome their wariness, and they will kiss (see the chapter 'The Couple's First Kiss') Maybe she regrets that first kiss, and tries to avoid getting too close to him again – that gives you scenes where she can't quite stop her eyes straying in his direction, she can still feel her lips tingling from the heat of his kiss, remembering how it felt.

And so, depending on the type of story you're writing, things will begin to escalate, the temperature rising with each scene. There will be more kisses – and they will start to wander, down into the sensitive spot at the base of her throat. And his hands will begin wandering too, brushing against the side of her breast, caressing the ripe swell, maybe even unfastening a few buttons and slipping inside to smooth over her bare skin.

How is she going to react to that? Maybe it's too soon, she barely knows him, she shouldn't be letting this happen. Maybe her desire is as urgent as his, but it's the wrong time, the wrong place – regretfully he has to step away. Maybe she's let it go further than she intended, and then overreacts, pushing him away angrily – and he taunts her that she seemed to have been enjoying it.

These moments will prompt both a physical and an emotional reaction – both at the time, and lingering in their memories.

In my novel *Chasing Stars,* Javier is watching the feed from the security cameras:

> *He wasn't specifically looking for her, of course. But there was no denying she looked pretty damn good in a plain dark blue swimsuit, wet and clinging to every delicious inch of her as she hauled herself up onto the swim-steps and squeezed the droplets of water from the long hank of copper curls hanging over her shoulder.*

> *And then... she hooked her fingers into the bottom of her swimsuit and ran them round over the smooth curve of her backside to ease the fabric back into place. Something hit him right in the solar plexus. It was a totally unconscious action, totally innocent and yet compellingly sensual.*

Sometimes, particularly if your romance is embedded within another genre, your lovers may sadly be kept apart for days, months or even years, perhaps with just a few snatched opportunities for a sight of each other or a few moments together. Maybe there will just be a letter, or a report that he was seen in the Southern Mountains. These tiny events will be treasured all the more, pored over in private – that letter will be tucked next to his heart, the folds wearing thin where he has re-read it so many times.

WHAT TO AVOID

Don't let the affair get too static or go round in circles. Remember the importance of story arc. Begin with small incidents, and fleeting reactions, and build the actions and responses with each encounter between your lovers.

RAYNE'S SUGGESTION

"Depending on the genre and the plot, the erotic tension between the characters may be intense or subtle, and it may play an important role in the relationship or a minor one. Think carefully about how much erotic tension is right for your book, your readers and your scene."

ASSIGNMENT

Shortly after your lovers' first physical encounter in your WiP – whether it's a touch, a kiss or whatever – your PoV character is trying to do something else which takes some concentration. Maybe holding a conversation with their boss or their mother, or trying to follow the instructions for a new piece of electronic equipment. But their memories of that encounter keep intruding. Write the scene, or part of it.

CHAPTER 21

CREATING EROTIC TENSION WITHOUT EROTIC ACTION

Rayne Hall

If you like, you can build erotic tension in your story without the characters doing anything sexual, by focusing on a character's desire.

The reader will feel the need, the hunger, the arousal as much as the character does. The resulting tension can be hotter than any actual sex.

Why would you do this?

- To heat up the story, the characters and the readers before sex takes place. (This is a great technique to use in Erotic Romance.)

- To drive a plot that's partly based on sexual desire, in which the relationship doesn't get consummated until after the book's end. (For example, both characters want to keep themselves pure for marriage, and the novel concludes with their engagement.)

- The character abstains from sex for moral, ethical, or spiritual reasons, and their need for chastity is part of the plot. By raising the sexual tension, you make it increasingly difficult to resist temptation, which makes the story more exciting and makes the reader root for the character. (For example, a character passionately desires a certain willing but married woman, and he fights against the temptation to commit adultery.)

TECHNIQUES

How do you create erotic tension if nothing remotely sexual occurs?

- Sex is forbidden. The character must not give in to temptation, or devastating consequences will happen. (If he has sex with that siren, his fiancée will leave him. If he has sex with that married woman, he will lose God's favour. If he has sex with that man, he'll have to acknowledge to himself that he is gay. If he has sex, he'll lose self-control and suck the woman's blood, turning her into a vampire....)

- The sex is in the character's mind. He fantasises about it – or better still, he fights to suppress those fantasies

- The desire is focused on one person, or one type of sex. The more specific the desire, the more intense the experience

- The character is very aware of the other person's physical presence. He notices a small detail – the little hairs on her arms, the mole at the corner of her mouth, the shape of her earlobe, the scent of her perfume. Describe that detail. Then have the character tear his thoughts away from that, seeking distraction. Then he notices another detail, tears himself away again

- An opportunity arises which would be perfect for sex. For example, he and the object of his desire accidentally meet in a deserted cottage. Nobody knows they're there, and nobody will ever find out. They have the whole night undisturbed. The woman is willing, indeed, she invites him into her bed... The character resists the temptation and sleeps on the couch in the living room, but he is aware of how wonderfully easy it would be right now. He can scarcely sleep all night. He hears her movements in the room next door, knows that she is waiting for him…

If you like, you can turn the erotic tension up so much that the reader is practically aflame with arousal. Beware, though: if you then allow the characters to consume the relationship, the sex (and the way you write it) must be phenomenal, otherwise it will be an anti-climax for the reader.

WHAT NOT TO DO

Don't turn up the sexual tension higher than appropriate for the genre. For example, if you write Inspirational Romance, your readers want a chaste book. Intense sexual tension between the characters would arouse the readers who don't wish to be aroused. For this type of book, introduce just mild sexual tension, just enough to show how the characters experience and resist temptation.

After building up enormous erotic tension, don't write a skimpy or bland sex scene. You need to follow it with either a phenomenal sex scene, or no sex at all. You've raised your readers' expectations, now you must fulfil them.

SUSANNE'S SUGGESTION

"The briefest touch can create a sizzle of heat – shaking hands on being introduced, passing a cup of coffee, helping her mount her horse. Even touching something she has worn – her glove, her scarf – will ignite erotic thoughts. This will be magnified the more the situation is inappropriate or the presence of other people force them to hide their reactions.

Any clue that the object of all this erotic desire feels the same way will set off a nuclear reaction! She becomes aware that his eyes are following her around the room, he notices that she lowers her eyes or nervously catches her lip between her teeth when he speaks to her. And when their eyes meet…!"

ASSIGNMENT

Write a paragraph in which the PoV character is physically aware of the other person's presence, and doesn't allow himself (or herself) to indulge in these thoughts.

CHAPTER 22

CLOTHING – AND HOW TO REMOVE IT

Susanne McCarthy

I know we're getting to the good bits, but before you can think about undressing your lovers you're going to have to backtrack a bit.

1. Character:

You've created these two people, and brought them to this point. Now all that characterisation is going to influence what happens next. Who are these two people? How much sexual experience do they each have?

Is one the classic alpha male, who is going to take control and who is effortlessly good at everything? Is the other feisty and challenging, giving as good as she gets? Or is she shy, inexperienced, lacking in confidence in her body? Is he a bit of rough, with tattoos and a motor-bike while she's a rather prim librarian? Is he the dynamic boss of a large corporation while she's his secretary, his cleaner – or maybe the boss of a rival company?

When you consider these factors it may seem obvious who has the power, and who is going to take the lead in the stripping stakes. But maybe not – it might be fun to turn it on its head. Maybe the librarian has a very vivid imagination, and this hunky biker is her chance to live out some of her steamy fantasies.

2. What has the relationship between them been like?

This is going to influence their mood, and to some extent the pacing of the scene. Have they been arguing a lot, and now suddenly the desire beneath the quarrelling has surfaced (though the reader knew a while back how they really felt.) Has he been openly intent on seducing her, while she has held him off – she's known too many guys like that in the past, and she doesn't want to fall for another one? Have they just faced terrible danger together, fought side by side, and suddenly his irritating habit of chewing on twigs doesn't matter anymore?

3. Where have they been immediately before the love scene, what have they been doing?

Have they been to a posh ball, where they have been dancing *very* close? Have they been arguing over the terms of a contract during a tense business meeting? Have they just defeated the great dragon Kraul and snatched the Sindril Stone?

4. Where are they now?

The opulent master bedroom in his fabulous apartment with its view of Sidney Harbour by night? The imposing boardroom of his company with the stern portraits of his father and grandfather gazing down at them? A narrow mountain cave, with the Sindril Guard hunting them?

5. What are they wearing?

Go back over the points above. What they are wearing will be influenced by the characters and what they have been doing – it's quite likely that you will have described their clothes in some detail.

Is he wearing biker leathers or a beautifully-tailored business suit? Is she wearing an elegant silk evening gown with narrow shoulder-straps, or a stolen suit of Sindril armour?

This is important, because you're going to have to think about how they're going to get these clothes off. You're also going to have to think of what they may be wearing underneath.

If you have them wearing something that's too complicated to get off (the leather straps on that Sindril armour can be so fiddly to undo!) maybe you need to slip in an extra scene to give them a chance to divest themselves of at least some of the awkward stuff.

Important historical note:

If you're writing a historical novel, you really need to do your research. Many readers, particularly fans of the Georgian/Regency/Victorian periods, know their costume history very well, and if you get it wrong you will pull them out of the story just at the crucial moment.

Do you know whether a dress would be laced at the back or the front? Would there have been buttons? Would the bodice be attached to the skirt, or separate? How were a man's shirt-cuffs fastened?

And crucially, what would they be wearing underneath? Do you know what it would have been made of – silk, cotton? Do you know whether they would have worn drawers?

And how on earth did you make love in a crinoline?

6. Fabrics

Think about how the fabrics will feel, how they will behave. Silk is cool and smooth, and slithers down over your skin. Cashmere is soft and warm and is also inclined to slither. A white cotton shirt may be crisp when fresh, but softens as it is worn. Other types of cotton are softer.

Raid your wardrobe to find a range of fabrics, then touch them, stroke them, let them glide across your bare arm. Write down the words that spring to mind. If you don't have the fabrics you want, it could be a good excuse to have a stroll round a fabric store or high-end clothes shop for a discreet fondle.

7. Fastenings

Long zips that can be slid down slowly, heavy duty zips on the fly of leather biker trousers. Lots of tiny pearl buttons that can be teasingly opened one by one – or ripped off impatiently. Studs and snaps which can be jerked apart. Lacings of ribbon or leather thongs which need to be slowly unravelled.

Belts – his or hers. With buckles that eager, clumsy fingers may fumble with. Belts that can be slid slowly out of belt-loops.

Velcro… er, maybe not. It's just not sexy, is it? (Although striptease performers use it to great effect!)

8. The disrobing

Are they going to remove their clothes themselves? Maybe she performs a provocative striptease for him, or he shrugs off his shirt as she watches? Or are they going to undress each other? Will it be a frenzied ripping of buttons, or a slow discarding of garments one by one?

Close your eyes and visualise them, in the setting you've placed them in, in the mood you've built up. Layer in some thoughts, dialogue and images to bring the scene to life.

Example 1:

He had discarded his jacket and tie, and unfastened his collar. She put up her hands against his chest, feeling the cool crispness of his white shirt beneath her fingers.

"Do you think your grandfather would mind?" she murmured, glancing up at the stern portrait on the wall of the boardroom.

"I don't care if he does."

"That's good." She smiled slowly as she unfastened the first button, then the second. Just at the base of his throat was a smattering of dark, curling hair. She unfastened the next button.

Example 2:

"In here. We have to hide."

"Let me see that arrow wound."

"It's nothing, just a scratch."

"Sindril arrows are sometimes poisoned. Will you lie still? Damn, these leather straps are so fiddly to undo."

Her fingers fumbled nervously with the buckles; the racing of her heart was no longer due to that desperate flight from the dragon's lair. At last all the buckles were unfastened. As he shrugged the armour off his wide shoulders the gleam of the second moonlight slanting into their narrow cave highlighted the smooth sculpting of his hard muscles...

9. And then... the underwear

Your alpha male probably isn't going to be wearing a vest, but your renegade Sindril warrior may well have on a linen undershirt to stop his armour rubbing. I doubt your successful businessman is going to be wearing greying Y-fronts or a red lurex thong. Looking back over many of my stories I realised I have a preference for navy silk-jersey boxers. Clinging and... yummy!

And what sort of lingerie is your lady wearing? Does your sensible librarian go for sensible white cotton? Bridget Jones big pants? Maybe she'll feel a stab of regret that she didn't go for black satin as his gaze roves hungrily over her body. But maybe he rather likes the innocent image she presents?

But on the other hand, maybe beneath that sensible pink cardigan and grey pinafore dress she is wearing luxurious French lace, with bra-cups which encase her full breasts enticingly. He's likely to remove her bra – he's probably going to be pretty good at that, though she doesn't want to think about how he learned to do it so deftly.

And her panties/briefs/knickers (delete according to preference.) Maybe lace-trimmed satin which he can slide down slowly over her slender thighs? Or rip off, if you prefer – she's not going to spare a moment's regret for their loss. Or maybe she will, and he'll laugh and promise her a new pair.

Or skip sections 5 to 9

Of course, you could always arrange for them to be wearing little or nothing in the first place – maybe they've been swimming, or got caught in a tropical rainstorm and have had to strip off their sopping wet clothes and change into dressing gowns or even a towel wrapped around his lean waist?

And it can be very erotic to leave them partially clothed, or even to have one of them naked while the other is fully dressed. From my novel *Christmas Secrets*:

> *He had moved on top of her, pinning her whole body beneath his. While she was naked, he was still fully clothed, and the soft abrasion of his jeans and sweater against her tender skin made her vividly aware of her feminine vulnerability to his hard male demand.*

WHAT TO AVOID

You don't have to describe the removal of every single item – some can easily be skipped, your lovers probably won't notice. I have written numerous scenes where shoes are heeled off or kicked off, where clothes are removed, but I don't recall ever mentioning him removing his socks. And my heroes are certainly never going to be the type to go to bed in their socks. Maybe the sock fairy comes along and twinkles them off his toes?

RAYNE'S SUGGESTION

"Clothing doesn't have to be removed to be sexy. What the other person wears can add to the attraction. It can even create tempting thoughts which the PoV character may or may not try to resist.

Imagine a pirate in white linen shirt, with the sleeves rolled up while he works on deck, revealing tanned, muscular arms. Maybe the top buttons of his shirt are open, and she gains a glimpse of his masculine, hairy chest.

Even in a 'chaste' story, you can use clothing to create enticing hints. Perhaps the hem of her skirt plays around her shapely calves as she walks."

ASSIGNMENT

In a scene for your WiP, describe the removal of one single item of clothing. (This could be a coat or scarf if you are writing a non-erotic piece.) Think about who removes it, how and why. What is the fabric, how does it feel to the touch? How is it fastened? (Even a simple scarf may be knotted or twisted around her neck.) How does each character feel as the item is removed?

CHAPTER 23

HOW TO WRITE EROTIC SCENES: SEEING, TOUCHING AND RESPONDING

Susanne McCarthy

This chapter and the chapter 'Getting Seriously Intimate' are mainly for writers of mainstream novels, both romance and where a romance is part of another genre, and for writers of erotic romance. Writers of Young Adult, religious-based or 'sweet' romances probably don't need to read any farther, and writers of erotica and BDSM (bondage, domination, sadism, masochism) probably don't need any advice from us!

This is the place where you gather together all the threads you have been weaving into your story: Who are your lovers? How did they come to this point? What do you have in store for them as they take the critical final steps towards commitment – what dangers or conflicts remain? And crucially, what is the nature of their relationship now? And what, for each of them, is their lovemaking style?

Now think about their immediate situation. What is the setting – the opulent bedroom of his penthouse apartment, a secluded cove on a Caribbean island, a narrow cave in a mountain pass? Have they snatched a few precious moments while escaping from the Sindril Guard, or do they have a whole long luxurious night ahead of them?

You are not writing a car maintenance manual. Erotic scenes are not about who puts what where. To quote one of the most famous erotica authors of all the time, Anaïs Nin, what you are aiming for is, "*A fusion of sexuality and feeling, sensuality and emotion.*"

Go back and look again at our chapter on 'The Couple's First Kiss'. How did you deal with those in your story? These are the same two lovers – a lot of how they felt and reacted then will be similar now.

Read the chapter on 'Clothing and How to Remove it', and start to think about how your lovers will get out of their clothes. Then you're already halfway there. Because of course love-making doesn't wait until they have their clothes off – the kissing, the disrobing, will all meld together to create the whole.

WHAT DO THEY SEE?

As they start to remove items of clothing, they will look at each other. What do they see? You will probably have collected images to help visualise your characters – now is the time to study the bodies, the muscles, the curves, the skin.

My favourite image for male bodies is Michelangelo's David – beautifully proportioned, with shoulders just wide enough, well-defined muscles in the arms and torso. I have my own little copy of it here in my workroom. You, of course, will have your own preferences. American writers often seem to like their heroes bulked-up a little more. Whatever you choose, what is your lady going to be thinking when she looks at him?

What is his skin like? Rarely pale, it will usually be sun-bronzed, gleaming gold, rich chocolate. Does he have tattoos or piercings? Does he have chest hair? I do like a smattering at the base of his throat or across his wide chest – some like it arrowing down into the waistband of his jeans. What is it going to feel like when your lady runs her fingers over it, or rests her cheek against it?

What about her body? Curves, slender or lush. Slim thighs, perhaps, a trim waist, a smooth stomach. Or maybe she's had a baby, and that has left its mark? What about what my mother used to call her "sit-upon" – her backside, buttocks, bum, derrière? Has she gone for the full Brazilian, or left the 'foliage' as nature intended?

Then there's the delicate subject of her breasts. Go on, you don't have to whisper it or call it a bosom – at least not in these circumstances. Full ones, small ones, pert ones… Think about the words you want to use – ripe swell, creamy curves, peach-like.

And the nipples – nubs and buds and rosebuds, berries and cherries, pink or crimson or chocolate, hardened or tender. Personally I'm not keen on having them 'thrusting' too much, even if they've already made their contours/outline known through her silky evening gown or wet swimsuit. And 'pebbling' – is that a thing?

Her skin, of course, will be smooth, satiny, creamy, golden, cinnamon-tinted, ebony – possibly even lightly freckled.

What is he going to be thinking when he looks at her? What is *she* going to be thinking when he looks at her? Is she a little shy, or body-confident? Is having him look at her an added turn-on? Have them notice and enjoy the contrast between them – his powerful maleness, with all those hard muscles, her soft feminine curves and satiny skin.

TOUCHING AND RESPONDING

There are going to be hands and mouths involved here, dancing fingertips and moist, hot, lapping tongues. But I can't remind you often enough that this isn't a matter of who puts what where; this is an interaction between two people who are falling in love. They are caressing each other, experiencing their own responses and being aware of their lover's responses. Enjoying their own pleasure but wanting their lover to enjoy it too.

And don't forget the hair. Mostly hers, long and silken and running through his fingers, or twisted around his hand. Cropped short, curly, smelling of the lemony shampoo she uses. And his hair – you've probably described it earlier, but how does it feel as she tangles her fingers in it?

And how does their skin smell? His own distinctive male smell, maybe slightly musky, a hint of fresh cologne? Hers maybe fresh, a hint of vanilla or tuberose, patchouli or Shalimar? Smell is a very powerful sense, it will drug your mind and always remind you of your lover. Months later she may find a shirt he has worn, and the memory will come back and pierce her heart.

Think of all the ways your lovers may touch each other. Gently, smoothly, caressing, stroking, kissing, trailing fingernails lightly over their lover's skin; roughly, nipping, biting, slapping. A bit playful, perhaps, or with heated urgency, desire.

How will it feel to touch like that? How will it feel to be touched like that? When he kisses the sensitive spot behind her ear or at the base of her throat? When she feels his hard muscles move beneath her hand, when he feels her supple body curved intimately close against his. What are they going to be thinking as they inch towards the intimacy they've both been vividly fantasising about?

Her breasts, of course, will receive a considerable amount of attention. In earlier scenes there may be caresses over her clothes – he may tease and tantalise, cup the ripe swell in his hand, brush his thumb over the ripening bud of her nipple. Then he might sneak his way inside – unfastening a few buttons or slipping up under her soft cashmere sweater – and do the same, maybe over her bra, maybe under.

And is she going to permit these liberties? That's going to depend on where they are on their trajectory towards the main event. If he's pushing a bit too fast she might push him away, blushing and furious as she straightens her clothes. Or she may be enjoying it – a *lot* – her head tipping back as she gasps for air?

Once they are seriously into the erotic action, he's likely to linger, stroking over her smooth skin, teasing her tender nipples into puckered peaks, perhaps there's a little light pinching. And kissing, swirling his hot tongue around the pink circles, nipping with his hard white teeth, drawing one deep into his mouth to suckle rhythmically.

There'll be sighs and soft moans, maybe a few husky-voiced comments. What does it do to his heart-beat, her pulse? Does she feel hot, light-headed, do her taut-strung nerve-fibres sizzle as if she's had an electric shock? He'll be feeling the growing tension inside him. The temperature is rising – short of some serious intervention, they are tripping past the point of no return. And they both know it – she feels her defences crumbling, he's aware of her surrender.

By the way, don't forget that he has sensitive spots too – and she may enjoy sending warning tremors through him as she strokes over his skin with her fingertip or her tongue. Including his nipples.

RAYNE'S SUGGESTION

"This is where you can use your own fantasies. Indulge in what the man of your dreams looks like with his shirt off, or remember what you used to fantasise about when you were the heroine's age. Write down what you see in your mind's eye, then tweak it to suit the characters and the plot."

FURTHER STUDIES

Consider *Writing Vivid Emotions* from the Writer's Craft series.

ASSIGNMENT

Start your own thesaurus of words and phrases you like to describe bodies, sensations and emotions. Use your imagination, look at Rayne Hall's book *Writing Vivid Emotions* and Bryn Donovan's *Master Lists for Writers*. Search through the writing of authors you enjoy and note what they use – copying odd words is not plagiarism, but copying whole sentences or paragraphs is a no-no.

CHAPTER 24

HOW EXPERIENCED ARE THE LOVERS?

Susanne McCarthy

Virgins are rarer in contemporary novels than they once were – to the point where if she is still a virgin, you may want to slip the reasons for this into her back-story. You will also need to decide whether or not she tells him, and why – and whether or not he believes her, and why. In historical novels it is more likely that your lady will be a virgin, unless of course that is part of your plot. That probably holds true for anything up to the 1950s.

Even if she isn't a virgin, it is likely that there will have been few previous lovers in her history (this often holds true even in erotic romances.) Perhaps they have betrayed her in some way. She may reflect on this when embarking warily on this enticing new love affair.

In my historical western novella *Rogan's Game*, Ella muses about her past:

> *The only thing she had of value was her reputation – a reputation that for a saloon girl teetered on a knife-edge. Yes, she had had lovers – but very few, and very discreet. A beau when she was seventeen, whose parents had sent him back east when they had found out he was seeing her; a rancher from Rawlins who had turned out to be married.*

The hero, on the other hand, is likely to have quite a bit of experience – that's *so* sexist, I know, but there it is. However, in the mainstream Romance genre at least, he will not be promiscuous – except maybe in a misspent youth which he has now left far behind. It's unlikely your alpha male will feel any performance anxiety, or if he does he certainly isn't going to admit it – even to you, though you're the one writing the story.

Of course, in erotic romances both partners may well have a *lot* of prior experience, but as in life it's not really polite to dwell on it.

Think about how these factors will influence the action. It's likely that the less experience she has, the more uncertain she will be – though instincts as old as Eve may inspire her to be more adventurous than she thought she dared. She may be anxious about what he may be thinking – maybe that he prefers women with more experience, or that he will realise she is in love with him.

If he is aware that she is a virgin, he is likely to be extra gentle, take it slowly – he is, after all, a gentleman. If he was unaware of it, or disbelieved it, he may be startled to discover it. (Look, I know that's not only sexist but probably medically inaccurate, but that's the way it rolls.) Maybe he tries to withdraw, but she stops him – with a word or an action. Of course, if it suits your plot you can have him not realise – no rules, remember?

How will he react? Hopefully, he will simply be happy that she trusted him enough. Or maybe he feels pride in it, regards it as a 'gift' or even some kind of victory – though this attitude is likely to be seen when it occurs early in your story, before the emotional progression you are going to write for him.

WHAT TO AVOID

In contemporary fiction we tend to recognise that a woman is more than her hymen, so don't make your lady too prissy about her virginity. Yes, it's quite a big deal but it's not on a par with the universe exploding. (OK, maybe on a par with a minor galaxy exploding in a historical piece or in some cultures – real or fantasy – especially if the couple aren't married.)

RAYNE'S SUGGESTION

Sexually inexperienced male lovers can be delightful, too. Have you read *Outlander* by Diane Gabaldon? This historical novel has a strong love story. Claire is experienced while her new husband Jamie is a virgin. Delicious!

ASSIGNMENT

In three sentences or less, write your lady's reflections on her prior sexual history.

CHAPTER 25

GETTING SERIOUSLY INTIMATE

Susanne McCarthy

A gentleman of finesse will never just dive in. The lady parts are very delicate – he will treat them as such. He'll take his time, maybe stroking slowly down her stomach, her thighs – and up again, over the silken smooth skin between, coaxing them a little apart. How is he feeling? Probably savouring the pleasure of finally having this woman naked in his arms, perhaps using all his will-power to restrain himself from rushing her.

How will she feel at this point? If she's inexperienced, she may feel nervous, vulnerable – in fact even if she's quite experienced, the first time with this man she's been crazy about for hours/weeks/years could possibly make her feel quite vulnerable. She's taking a risk, surrendering to him both physically and emotionally. Has she judged him, his feelings, his intentions, accurately? If not, she could to be in for a lot of heartache and self-reproach tomorrow.

But there'll also be also excitement, anticipation. The touch of his fingers on the soft, tender folds could make her shiver with heat, the brush of his thumb over the exquisitely sensitive nub of pleasure makes her gasp, breathe more rapidly, her blood rushing through her veins. And when he gently slips his finger deep inside her...

And then – maybe shocking her a little – he kisses his way down over her smooth stomach, maybe diverting for a moment around her navel, then down... and when his hot tongue takes over what his fingers have been doing, the sensations are delicious as she parts her thighs invitingly...

GIVING HEAD

It's a truth universally acknowledged that men just *love* to have a woman (or a man, if preferred) give them head. But many women like it too – not necessarily the act itself, but the idea of giving their man pleasure in such a tenderly intimate way. They like the sexual power of it, taking the initiative, teasing and tantalising him – maybe dotting butterfly kisses down over his stomach and thighs, or letting her hair stroke across his taut arousal as if by accident.

Then she'll swirl the hard shaft with her tongue, around it and down the length. As she takes it between her lips she might slant a few wicked glances up at him. And he's watching her, his breathing ragged, powerful tremors shuddering through him.

You may choose to linger over this, especially if you are writing an erotic romance. There are many interesting things she may do, some of which could send him crashing through the ceiling (for more, Google 'fellatio' – there are even online tutorials!) She may even be able to do the 'deep throat' thing – not many people can, so that's going to be a bit special.

Is she going to stop as she feels the approaching peak of his arousal, and continue in the more conventional way, or is she going to finish what she's started, to give him the most exquisite moment of ecstasy? And if she's really into this, she'll probably swallow the gush of slightly salty liquid – for reasons none of them seem able to explain, men really love this.

PRACTISING SAFE SEX

A brief pause before we plunge (ooops, sorry!) on. He – or maybe she – has a condom (or several). Of course they do – our lovers are sensible adults and practice safe sex. They may wonder about the convenience of its appearance, they may even ask about it or tease about it. But they use it – them. (Unless a pregnancy or STD is part of your plot.)

You don't have to use the word "condom" if you feel it's too clinical. Sheath – or even silken sheath. Or protection. It'll be pretty clear what you're talking about.

It doesn't have to interrupt the action, it can be part of it. Even if the wrapper is a bit tricky to open (strong white teeth again!) He can put it on, or she can – rolling it slowly over the hard shaft of his arousal can be *very* sensual. She might be teasing him with her eyes as she does it. If she's extremely clever she can put it on with her mouth. I'm not sure how that works, so you'll have to go and research it for yourself. (In books. Of course in books.)

You don't need to be specific about what happens to it afterwards. A gentleman always disposes of it discreetly.

THE MAIN EVENT

Finally. Well, maybe one or both of them has had a main event already, what with all that touching and mouths and stuff, but this is the *main* main event.

It may seem redundant at this point – maybe he should have checked sooner? – but this is the latest moment to make sure this is consensual. His growl of, "Is this what you want?" Her breathless, "Yes, please, more…"

You've placed them in a setting, so use it – the satin sheets beneath her naked body, the hard edge of the boardroom table, the prickly warmth of a pile of hay. (Do you know, research indicates that only one in a hundred couples make love on the stairs? What a pity – you can be very imaginative with stairs!) Maybe they're in the shower with warm water pouring down over their naked bodies – or maybe outside their cosy cave it's pouring with rain, the heavy drops pattering loudly on the rocks (at least that should hold up the Sindril Guard for a while.)

Don't worry too much about describing positions – standing up or lying down are probably sufficient. And if lying down, most people will probably visualise the missionary position – don't underestimate it, it allows plenty of visual contact and interaction, which is what you want. If you are going to have several erotic episodes, you can consult the *Kama Sutra* and throw in some variations later.

Get out the thesaurus you've been working on. Does she yield to him, surrender? Open to him, take him? Does he take her? There's movement – rhythmic, smooth, slow, hard, fast, thrusting, driving, an ancient dance. There's gasping, dragging for breath, spines curving. There may be a little dialogue – encouragement, pleading for more. There will be physical responses – bones melting, heat pooling like molten gold, spinning vortexes and metaphorical fireworks – before they finally collapse, exhausted in each other's arms.

And there's an emotional impact. Remember, your lovers have been building up to this through hate and love, storms and danger, resistance and interference and delays. Don't rush them, let them linger over it – even if the Sindril Guard are after them and they have to be over the mountain pass by morning.

It's a *big deal*. Make it count.

WHAT TO AVOID

Don't neglect the emotional aspect of the love-making. Remember, you're writing a love scene, not pornography.

RAYNE'S SUGGESTION

"Remember the characters' personalities, experiences, habits and hang-ups, and let them surface during the most intimate moments.

When you've written a section of sex, imagine different characters in the same action. Would they say and do the same things in the same way? Then the draft is not good enough. Scrap it and start over.

The mark of a good sex scene is that it's personal to the specific characters.

Before the couple have sex, make sure they both give their consent. Your readers will feel better if there is no room for doubt.

In 1970s romance novels, the heroine sometimes said "no" but he knew that she really meant "yes" and proceeded. And sometimes he took her by force against her will, to demonstrate what a masterful man he was, and then her cries of protest turned into moans of lust. Today's readers would find this behaviour unacceptable.

To ensure that your readers know that the characters have given full consent, add a little dialogue. One can ask "Are you sure you want this?" and the other replies, "Yes. Oh, yes please." Then you're safe, and your readers will relax and enjoy themselves."

ASSIGNMENT

Choose the setting – perhaps an unusual setting, or even the stairs – and decide what the lovers are going to do. Write a brief summary of the action. You can flesh it out in sensual words later.

CHAPTER 26

HOW NOT TO MAKE YOUR READERS SPLUTTER

Susanne McCarthy

It's very easy to get erotic scenes horribly wrong. Remember that you are writing about two people who are falling madly in love with each other (or perhaps renewing their love.) You aren't writing a car maintenance manual.

"Sex loses all its power and magic when it becomes explicit, mechanical, overdone." Anaïs Nin.

What does a bad erotic scene look like? Since 1993, the Guardian Literary Review's Bad Sex in Fiction Award has honoured authors who have produced an outstandingly bad scene of sexual description in an otherwise good novel. Google it – but put your coffee cup down first or you could make a terrible mess of your keyboard.

What can we learn from this?

- Be careful with your similes and analogies – you could conjure images you didn't intend

- Don't let your metaphors wander too far from what your lovers are doing – getting carried away with descriptions of wild thunderstorms or stampeding mustangs could cause your reader to lose the thread

- Be careful how you describe the various essential body parts – don't go overboard trying to find something original. You'd probably want to avoid medical terms, and in a mainstream romance the words should not be too explicit – in erotic romance those are more acceptable

- It's a matter of personal taste, but some words are just a turn-off. For me, that's "tumescence" and "bulbous." Breasts could be described as being like ripe peaches, but "globes" suggests the addition of copious amounts of silicone

- Speaking of fruit, that's OK (probably not vegetables.) But use it with restraint.

Think about how you will name the intimate body parts. Consider your intended readership. What kind of words will they prefer? While erotic romances can be merrily littered with explicit vernacular terms (both male and female 'c' words for example) mainstream writing tends to avoid those, and go for similes and metaphors.

RAYNE'S SUGGESTION

"Almost any erotic description can incite some readers to giggle. What some readers find arousing, others find silly. So there is no clear guideline about what words to use or not to use. Susanne's tips will be helpful in avoiding the most awkward phrases, but bear in mind that your readers' tastes may differ."

ASSIGNMENTS

Go and have another look at those bad sex writing awards, a dire warning. Then work on your thesaurus again. How are you going to refer to the… um… male member? Tension, hardness, arousal? Shaft? Is it long, thick? (If you find a bulbous tumescence in there, attack it immediately with a red pen.)

And the lady parts? You can have secret core, velvet folds, rosy petals, but do try to avoid anything too florid. And it can be moist, even wet – just don't get too squidgy. And then there's that thing – you know, the exquisitely sensitive thing, the focus of all her taut-strung nerve-fibres, the hidden seed-pearl of pleasure.

Read aloud a critical scene from your WiP. Maybe – if you're brave enough – read it to someone else. If any phrase gives rise to unintended laughter or cries of "neughhh!" cross it out.

CHAPTER 27

PLACING EROTIC SCENES IN YOUR PLOT

Susanne McCarthy

In many mainstream romances, or where the romance is part of another genre, there may only be one scene of erotic action, which will often come towards the end of the story, after a long build-up of erotic tension. The partners will usually be in love before the scene – at least, the reader will know they are, even if they don't know it themselves yet.

But that's not a rule. There may be several scenes of erotic action which come earlier, even at the beginning – 'secret baby' and 'coerced marriage' stories often follow this pattern.

In erotic romance there will be a lot more sexual activity from the beginning, and the woman will usually be a very active participant, even the instigator of the action. The sex may precede the falling in love, but characterisation and plot are still important, and there will still be the Happy-Ever-After.

However you approach it, you need to make sure that the erotic action comes in the right place for *your* lovers – that it fits realistically with their characters and what is happening in your plot. If you're struggling at this point, it may be that your characters are trying to tell you that they're not ready for this yet. Read back over what you've written – you may need to ramp up the heat a little by tweaking the dialogue or adding some more thoughts and reactions. Or you may need a whole extra scene or two.

BUT: The big erotic scene is not the end of the matter, even when it comes towards the end of the story. Readers enjoy that last little bit of tension. So even as your lovers are recovering their breath in a tangle of sheets, they haven't yet voiced their final commitment to each other.

WHAT TO AVOID

They don't *have* to have kissed before the big scene – maybe they've had a couple of near-misses? But if they've been squabbling for two hundred pages without showing any signs of being attracted to each other, it's going to be a bit of a jolt if they suddenly jump each other's bones.

This doesn't mean that it can't happen quite suddenly, particularly if they are in a dangerous situation – it's well known that danger can heighten sexual awareness (why do you think your teenage boyfriend used to take you to horror films?) Or maybe they have been squabbling since they met, but the temperature has been rising and suddenly it boils over.

RAYNE'S SUGGESTION

"Sometimes it's effective to delay erotic scenes. Don't allow the couple to go to bed together yet, however much they want to. Perhaps they must wait until they get married, perhaps one of them doesn't feel ready yet, or perhaps they're about to have sex when the book's villain bursts into the bedroom with a gun. While delaying the actual sex scenes, you can keep increasing the erotic tension."

ASSIGNMENTS

1. In your WiP, find three changes you could make to the dialogue before the big erotic scene to ramp up the heat.

2. In your WiP, think of an extra scene you could add which shows one or both of your lovers feeling the powerful tug of attraction, temptation.

CHAPTER 28

KEEPING THE BEDROOM DOOR CLOSED – HOW TO IMPLY INTIMACY WITHOUT SHOWING IT

Rayne Hall

Does the plot require the couple to have sex, but you don't want the reader to share their intimate moments? Then you can metaphorically 'close the bedroom door' and simply let the reader know what is going on.

Many new writers believe that they need to write graphic sex. But not all readers want that. Many prefer stories in which the bedroom door remains discreetly closed. For this type of story, the characters don't need to be chaste – but they don't act out their intimate passions in front of an audience.

If this approach would suit your novel and your readers, here are some techniques to make it work.

SKIP TO THE NEXT SCENE

The smoothest way is to end the scene shortly before the characters get intimate, and to begin the next scene after they've finished.

For example, Scene A plays out in the evening in her flat, where couple enjoy the lovely candlelit dinner she's prepared. Scene B opens with the man coming out of the shower in her flat and cooking breakfast, wearing nothing but a towel wrapped around his hips.

This feels natural, and the reader knows that the two spent the night together.

If you like, you can plant additional hints. For example, you can mention in Scene A that her flat doesn't have a guest room, and describe in Scene B the warm glow filling her whole body.

WHAT IS THE SEX LIKE?

If the intimacy is important for the relationship or the story, your readers need to know what it was like. You can convey this without graphic descriptions, and without even mentioning sex.

My favourite method is to let the couple share a meal before they become intimate. Show how they eat: Do they devour the food hungrily, or do they eat slowly, savouring every morsel? Who takes the initiative? Does one serve the other, or does each try to provide enjoyment for their partner?

You can use this method to hint at harmony or at conflict. For example, if you want to indicate that the man is impatient and inconsiderate, you can show him starting to eat at once before she's ready, and helping himself without offering the dish to her. If you show how he takes most of the dessert for himself, the reader understands that the sex that follows will not be a rewarding experience for her, and that the relationship is not going to be as loving as she had hoped.

If dinner doesn't fit the plot, you can also use a meal afterwards – for example, breakfast – and apply the same techniques.

Food-sharing works best as a metaphor for intimacy, but if this doesn't suit your story, use whatever action fits the plot, e.g. they may be bandaging each other's wounds after the battle.

WHAT NOT TO DO

The use of '…' in place of intimate action is outdated and clumsy, and can leave readers irritated.

SUSANNE'S SUGGESTION

"Maybe she wakes up and lies there watching him sleep, thinking about what happened last night – in general or specific terms. From my novella *Rogan's Game*:

> *Ella lay in bed, gazing out of the window, savouring the warm ache in her body. Beside her, Josh was still sleeping, that long, strong body naked against hers. It had been quite a night – unforgettable.*

Maybe she wakes up to find him gone – this may be expected or unexpected, he may be in the next room or the next continent. But there's a hollow in the pillow, and the scent of his skin lingering on the bedclothes.

Their subsequent dialogue may also refer to it. He may tease her about being shy after what has happened, he may remind her that her 'butter-wouldn't-melt-in-her-mouth' act won't wash anymore."

ASSIGNMENT

If the couple in your novel have sex and you don't want to show it graphically, imagine what their intimacy will be like. Write a few sentences describing how they share a meal before they make love. Each sentence should tell the reader something about the attitude and actions that will happen behind the closed bedroom door.

CHAPTER 29

KEEPING YOUR CHARACTERS AND LOVE SCENES CHASTE

Rayne Hall

Are you writing a 'clean read' or 'sweet romance'? Readers choose this kind of book because they don't want to be sexually aroused by what they read. Honour your readers' trust, and respect their wish.

This means you have to protect not just the story characters' chastity, but the reader's.

WHAT MAKES A CHASTE SCENE?

- The characters don't engage in any sexual action – not even hot embraces and passionate kisses

- The characters don't get sexually aroused. (It's your responsibility as an author not to put them into arousing situations.)

- The characters don't think about sex. (They don't fantasise about the other naked, and don't yearn for each other physically.)

- The characters aren't aware of each other as sexual beings. (This aspect can be tricky, so I'll address it later on in this chapter.)

- The readers don't perceive the characters as sexual beings

- The readers don't imagine the characters having sex

- The readers don't get sexually aroused by reading. (Reading can inflame sexual desires, and to a reader who's not used to erotic content, even the mildest suggestion can be arousing.)

TECHNIQUES

Here are practical tips how to keep a love scene chaste without sacrificing vividness and realism.

- Don't provide detailed descriptions of the characters' bodies. You can use a word to give a broad idea of their body shape – for example, *plump, petite, slender, wiry, stocky, athletic, tall* – but don't describe how her calves curve and how the jeans hug his narrow hips

- When the characters touch, use the vocabulary carefully, and don't go into detail. When he holds her in his embrace, or when she lays a hand on his arm, describe the emotional rather than the physical effect. Choose words like *tender, steadying, calming, supportive, encouraging, warm, comforting*

- Now for the tricky part: how to avoid sexual awareness between the lovers. Two people who're in love or who view each other as prospective spouses, are naturally aware of each other as sexual beings. Denying that would give your scene an unrealistic tone. The solution is to acknowledge the awareness, but not to dwell on it. From the PoV character's perspective, show a small physical detail of the other person. Use positive but not sensual language for this. (Examples: *Golden freckles danced on her arm. His biceps bulged under the heavy load.*) Then immediately focus on something else. This reflects how chaste people deal with physical thoughts: they redirect their attention

- If the plot requires that the characters are tempted, show the PoV deliberately shutting off that line of thought, and distracting himself and the other person by focusing on something else. *(Example: Golden freckles danced on her arms, like sprinkles of sunlight on tanned skin… He pulled his gaze away. "Time to launch the boat. Are you ready?")*

- Perhaps only one of the characters is tempted to indulge in a sensual experience. Then the other takes responsibility for both and disengages gently and tactfully, so the withdrawal doesn't feel like a rejection. (Example: *She melted against him, her heart thudding in her chest. She tilted her face upwards and opened her lips. Gently, he pushed her away. "Time to launch the boat. Are you ready?" His voice was tender, his smile warm.*)

WHAT NOT TO DO

If you're writing a 'clean' book, don't deviate from this in love scenes for the sake of misguided realism. Respect your readers' wishes, and keep the characters and the story chaste.

SUSANNE'S SUGGESTION

"Your characters may kiss, but it would be a light, chaste kiss. It might well be on the forehead or cheek, rather than the lips. It could be the barest touch, like a butterfly's wings – use words like warm, soft, tender. Even if on the lips it won't involve tongues or any suggestion of 'French' kissing.

There may be some hesitation about it, or it may be impulsive – or both. And as Rayne suggests, both you and your characters then move swiftly on:

He hesitated, then bent his head and brushed his lips lightly over hers. "Merry Christmas."

Follow this with a sentence about something else – perhaps an action or a line of dialogue. This should be a change of subject, but arise naturally from the current situation."

ASSIGNMENT

Choose an innocuous physical detail the PoV observes in the other person. Write a sentence describing it in an attractive, but not sexual way.

CHAPTER 30

HOW TO STIR YOUR READER'S EMOTIONS

Rayne Hall

A reader who feels moved by a scene will keep thinking about it, will mention it to others, and will remember it for a long time, perhaps for the rest of her life. If you arouse strong emotions in your readers, they'll want more books by the same author.

Love scenes are a great place to stir the reader's emotions.

Here are my four favourite techniques for achieving this.

1. **Get deep into the Point-of-View character's experience.**

This is the most important method. The reader experiences events through the filter of the PoV character. This means that you share only what's inside that one character's head and heart.

If you handle this skilfully, what the PoV feels is what the reader feels.

You may want to re-read the chapter 'Immersing the Reader: Point-of-View'.

2. **Use visceral responses.**

Instead of telling the reader how the character feels, describe the physical effects of the emotion. Where in the body does the character feel this, and how does this feel?

Instead of

He felt nervous.

Write

His insides quivered.

Instead of

She felt grateful.

Write

Her whole body tingled with warmth.

Instead of

She felt happy.

Write

A wave of warmth washed through her, and her heart danced.

Instead of

He felt love.

Write

His heart banged and his abdomen fluttered.

If you're not sure how to describe the emotion viscerally, think back to a time when you felt something similar. Recall the memory as vividly as you can, and observe how it affects your body.

Show visceral reactions only to what the PoV-character feels.

3. Use smells.

No other sense evokes emotions as strongly as the sense of smell. Two kinds of smells work especially well in love scenes – the fragrance of the place, and the partner's scent.

In a love scene, it's best to use only pleasant smells. Avoid unpleasant odours.

Describe the fragrance of the place the moment the PoV character gets there. For example, mention the smell of burning wood the moment she enters the room where the log fire burns, and the lavender-scented sheets the moment she sinks into the bed.

The right time to describe the partner's scent is when the two get close enough to smell it. For example, he may smell of horses and leather, and when they get closer still she becomes aware of lemony cologne and masculine sweat.

4. **Trigger the reader's own memories.**

Readers respond most strongly when what happens in the book evokes an emotional situation from their own life.

A reader who has been tormented by jealousy will relate to a character who suffers the same. If she had to decide whether to risk everything in order to be with the man she loves, she'll feel empathy with the character who has to make a similar choice.

Whatever situation your love scene describes – the heady excitement of a first date, the pain of a break-up, a heart-wrenching sacrifice or passionate arousal – try to write it in a way that it reminds the reader of their own experiences.

This way, the reader will feel not just what's on the page, but what she herself has felt in the past.

WHAT NOT TO DO

Don't tell the reader how the character feels. Show it.

SUSANNE'S SUGGESTION

"The strongest emotions are often best conveyed by the lightest touch. We all enjoy a good tear-jerker, but it can be irritating to feel we are being jerked too hard. Sometimes you don't even need to describe the emotions directly. You have put your characters in this situation – now just leave them there for a moment, and allow your reader to pour their own emotions into the space.

In my novel *Chasing Stars,* Kat and Javier were on a secluded beach when a manipulative teenager shows up and drags Javier away...

Leaving his casual fling behind with the debris of their picnic lunch, to be collected when convenient."

FURTHER STUDY

If you want to get deeper into this subject, you may find my guide *Writing Vivid Emotions* useful.

ASSIGNMENTS

1. For the love scene you're writing or revising, craft one sentence describing a pleasant fragrance. Decide where to insert it.

2. What is the PoV-character's most intense emotion in this scene? Craft a sentence showing how it feels viscerally.

CHAPTER 31

LAYERING LOVE SCENES WITH OTHER SCENES

Rayne Hall

Consider combining the love scene with another scene you've already planned or drafted. If other events play out at the same time as the lovers' interaction, drama and tension increase, and the scene won't be drenched in sentimentality.

Think of an exciting (perhaps even thrilling) external plot.

Perhaps they fall in love while working together rescuing earthquake victims. Or perhaps the police officer proposes marriage to his colleague while a crazed criminal is trying to kill them.

If none of the planned plot events is a good match, simply give your characters an urgent, important and difficult task to accomplish in the scene.

Of course, this 'layering' method doesn't suit every plot, but if it does, you'll get a dynamic scene that holds the reader in breathless excitement.

THE BEST LAYERING TECHNIQUE

The two plot strands play out simultaneously, and both involve the PoV character and his lover. Switch the focus between the two layers, while keeping both alive. When's the best moment to switch to the other layer?

- Whenever there's a lull in the 'external action' plot strand and the tension eases (for example, they've succeeded in freeing the child trapped under the rubble, or the crazed killer has stopped shooting at them), bring the love strand into the foreground

- Whenever the tension in the love strand is at its highest (not when it's low!), let the external action cut in. For example, he's about to propose marriage when they hear a scream from a collapsed building. Or maybe she's about to confess her true identity at last, when a bullet pings above their heads and they must dive for cover

Remember: high tension in love strand > switch to external plot. Low tension in external plot > switch to love plot.

This is the ideal pattern, but it's not a rule. If it works for your scene, great. But if it's not a good fit, don't force it.

WHAT NOT TO DO

Don't devote a whole scene exclusively to sweet talk or love-making, unless those are plot-changing and dramatic in their own right.

SUSANNE'S SUGGESTION

"If you are writing in the Romance genre there may not be tense or dangerous scenes arising out of your plot, but there would be lots of opportunities within your story to put your lovers together in circumstances where they may be interacting, but that is not the primary activity in the scene:

- At a dinner party, a charity ball, a sports event

- In a professional meeting – a board-meeting, a team briefing at the start of a shift or drug-raid

- With a child around – a squalling baby that urgently needs a nappy change, a curious tweenager asking innocently awkward questions, a sulky adolescent

The presence of other people, maybe the need to interact with other people or to concentrate on what is going on will add a layer of complexity. The presence of the lover may be an irritating distraction – or the other people may be the irritation.

The need to conceal their feelings will cause emotional churn. And *ooops!* they may get caught out – they miss a question, or take a wrong turning."

FURTHER STUDY

If you want to learn more about novel plotting, *Writing Vivid Plots* from the Writer's Craft series may be a good choice for you.

ASSIGNMENTS

1. What other plot events could happen at the same time?

2. Visualise both layers playing out – the love plot and the external action plot.

3. Identify at least one 'high tension' moment in the love plot. This is where the outside events will jolt the characters out of their romantic interlude.

Identify at least one 'low tension' moment in the external plot. This is when the two characters become emotionally aware of each other.

CHAPTER 32

ADD SUBTLE SOUND EFFECTS: EUPHONICS

Rayne Hall

Certain sounds have certain effects on the psyche. By using words which include those sounds, you influence how the reader feels.

This is an advanced technique and best used for revising a draft.

Apply the sounds with a light brush, like subtle make-up. The reader should not be aware of the technique, only feel the results.

Here are some sounds to intensify the mood of your love scene.

'M' FOR COSY COMFORTS

The 'M' sound is warm, gentle, homely, welcoming. In the English language, many words conveying this mood contain the letter 'M', for example: *comfort, mild, merciful, mollycoddling, mulled, mellow, warmth, amiable, embrace, home, comfort, ambience, meal.*

Use these words, and others containing the 'M' sound, whenever you want to convey a sense of cosiness, comfort and safety.

The 'M' also represents female-ness, especially of a mature motherly kind: *mother, mum, mammal, maternal, madonna, moon, mare, womb.*

Here are some other words with 'M' sounds you can use to add to the effect, although their meaning is unrelated: *mean, mush, meek, humble, arm, harm, market, mirth, merry, mask, mantle, mill, mouse, amble, ample, amber.* Of course there are many more words with 'M'. Simply pick the ones which suit your scene.

'P' FOR MASCULINITY

Words including the 'P' sound, especially those beginning with 'P', convey a sense of masculinity.

Indeed, the English language has many words which suggest maleness, such as *patriarchy, paternal, progenitor* – and quite a few which represent the male sexual organ or are have a phallic shape: *penis, prick, priapic, pillar, post.* Words representing penetration also often start with 'P': *poke, pierce, prong, push.*

When you want to emphasise maleness in your scene – perhaps while describing the handsome hero's masculine physique – include a few words with the 'P' sound.

Here are some words to get your creativity flowing. Of course, the English language has many more. *apply, park, perk, pug, puppy, posy, plug, apple, pear, grape, apricot, peach, painting, portrait, picture, people, ping, peg, gape, lip, ship, pen, pulse, parchment, palaver, ploy, ape, sap, tap, sip, tip, pillow, pirouette, pry, pray, staple, pry, ploy, slip, plant, peek, peer, nape, plate, platinum, planet, ship, rip, spin, wasp, lamp, ample, shape, priest, pride, pomp, prudent, pay, play, pose, possess.*

'L' FOR LINGERING PLEASURES

When your characters are in a relaxed, playful mood – perhaps even engaged in leisurely foreplay – use the 'L' sound. It is a sound of sensuality and unhurried pleasure.

Many 'L'-words in the English language convey this mood: *leisure, pleasure, idle, pliant, loll, relax, play, lie, lazy, linger, lick, luscious, lips, slow, mellow, lie, pleasant, pillow, laid-back, sensuality, lap, tickle, leer, lecherous, lips, labia, lesbian, lascivious, lust.*

The 'L' sound can also serve to convey female-ness, especially when contrasted with the male 'P'.

Here are some other words you can add to increase the effect: *laugh, chuckle, long, languish, language, lurid, pale, shell, wall, pile, plunder, pill, melon, light, lad, loud, delay, last, yellow.*

WHAT NOT TO DO

On discovering this technique, inexperienced writers often get carried away and overdo it. They cram so many euphonic words into their sentences that the effect is not subtle but ridiculous.

Remember to use euphonics sparingly, so your readers don't consciously notice the technique. To manipulate the reader's subconscious, you need to be subtle.

SUSANNE'S SUGGESTION

"Rhythm is related to euphonics. The length of a sentence can underpin a mood. Short sentences convey edginess, anxiety, anger. Long sentences are particularly evocative in an erotic scene, where they convey smooth, languid movements and slowly mounting tension which tips over into a breathless climax along with your lovers."

FURTHER STUDY

To learn more about how euphonics can influence the reader's subconscious, you may want to study my book *Euphonics for Writers.*

ASSIGNMENTS

1. Identify a paragraph or section in your scene where you want to convey cosy comfort, masculinity or leisurely sensuality. Make a list of words containing the relevant sound, which might fight into context.

2. Add a few words. Read the paragraphs aloud to see if you like the effect. Remember not to overdo it.

CHAPTER 33

WHAT TO CONSIDER WHEN WRITING LOVE SCENES IN DIFFERENT GENRES

Rayne Hall

Different genres require different treatment of love scenes. Here are some suggestions. These are just guidelines, not rules. Genre boundaries have become more fluid than they used to be, and authors may deviate from the norm if it serves the story.

ROMANCE

In a Romance novel, almost every scene is a love scene, carrying the relationship between the two characters forward. The scenes come in a given order, and it's best to stick to this with only minor variations, or you'll risk disappointing your readers (and having your novel rejected by publishers).

Typically, the first scene is the first meeting between the two lovers. They are instantly attracted to each other, but fight the attraction. Several scenes may feature misunderstandings and the characters resolving them, as well as serious reasons (such as conflicting loyalties) that keep them apart.

Around two thirds into the novel comes a dramatic climax scene, often involving one of the characters rescuing the other, and then both temporarily setting aside their differences as a team. For this scene, consider using a dramatic or dangerous setting. (The chapter

'Choosing the Location' contains a section with tips for dramatic and dangerous settings.)

The last scene of the novel is usually a 'final commitment' scene, when the couple have resolved their conflicts and pledge to spend the future together. In this scene, you need to convince the reader that this couple have not only found solutions for the conflicts and problems that plagued them through the book, but that they are able solve all future problems that life will throw at them. For tips on how to write such a scene (see the chapter 'Final Commitment – And Perhaps a Proposal of Marriage').

Sometimes there is an 'epilogue' with a short love scene showing the couple several years later, happily together. This epilogue love scene typically takes place in cosy surroundings (use the techniques shown in the chapter 'Choosing the Location'), proves that they have truly overcome what once kept them apart, and may feature them as a happy family with children.

In the next chapter Susanne will share professional tips on how to write love scenes for some specific subgenres of Romance.

HUMOUR

Love scenes in the Humour genre often involve misunderstandings. Create chuckles by constantly switching between what the reader expects and the unexpected.

FANTASY

The love story subplot in Fantasy novels often involves conflicting loyalties. The characters have to make tough choices. Often they either sacrifice their loyalties for their love, or their love for their loyalty, with heart-wrenching consequences. You'll find advice on handling this in the chapter 'Sacrifice for Love'.

In the Fantasy genre, the lovers often belong to different cultures, or even to different species. In Chapter 'Different Cultures, Different Species' I show how to write about this.

The level of erotic tension and action in Fantasy varies between the subgenres. The lovers in Epic Fantasy are often chaste (with no sexual action between them), and if they have sex, it is implied rather than graphic. For ideas how to imply sex without showing it, see the chapter 'Keeping the Bedroom Door Closed: How To Imply Intimacy Without Showing It'. The tension is emotional rather than erotic. (However, some works of Epic Fantasy feature sex scenes.)

In Urban Fantasy, on the other hand, sex often plays a role in the plot. The erotic tension may mount, and the characters may engage in sex, whether on the page or behind closed doors.

SCIENCE FICTION

In Science Fiction, the lovers often belong to different cultures, and occasionally are even of different species. The chapter 'Different Cultures, Different Species' can help with this.

The Space Opera subgenre tends to have sex scenes, while the Hard Science Fiction subgenre is often sex-free.

The relationship frequently ends with one of the lovers departing to a destination so far away that they will never meet again, so your story probably includes a break-up scene. For guidance, read the chapter 'Breaking Up'.

HORROR

In the Horror genre, the romantic subplot serves to break up the unrelenting terror by interspersing moments of comfort, respite and hope.

The two lovers may not like each other initially, and may not feel attracted to one another, but as the world around them falls apart, they realise that sticking together is their best chance of survival. In this situation, they become allies and gradually fall in love. The chapter 'Forming a Reluctant Alliance' will help you write these scenes.

Sometimes, one lover will sacrifice himself to give the other a chance of survival. Such final moments are brief and heart-wrenching for the reader. See the chapter 'Sacrifice for Love' for advice on how to write this scene.

THRILLER

The two characters may not like each other much at first, but working for a shared cause – get justice, find the serial killer before he strikes again – brings them close. In the early scenes, even though they may resent having to work together, they come to appreciate the other's skills and qualities. Gradually, they learn that they can depend on each other.

The advice in the chapter 'Forming a Reluctant Alliance' may suit those scenes. Often, erotic tension builds between the two, but they don't have sex. They may want to, but there never is the time.

Similarly, they may not express their growing affection for each other, because they're so busy chasing the killer that there never is a right moment.

During the novel's Climax, there's often a scene in which one character is in peril and the other comes to his rescue. The plan fails, and both are at the mercy of the sadistic villain. In this terrifying situation, with their lives in jeopardy, they may finally say, "I love you." For this scene, use a dangerous setting and with tips from the chapters 'Choosing the Location' and 'Lovers Talking: Dialogue'.

COSY MYSTERY

In this genre, the characters are attracted to each other, but cautious, because the other is a murder suspect. Of course she doesn't believe that he did it – but she needs to exercise caution, so she hides her feelings. Love scenes in Cosy Mysteries are tentative, courteous, without a major display of emotions. They rarely involve erotic tension, and if sex takes place, it happens behind closed doors. The chapter 'Keeping the Bedroom Door Closed: How To Imply Intimacy Without Showing It' can be useful for this.

YOUNG ADULT

Young Adult (teenage fiction) used to be sex-free, with not as much as a hint of erotic desires. Given the hormonal turmoil most teenagers go through, this is unrealistic. Modern YA therefore includes some erotic tension and sometimes erotic action, but it's probably best not to take it too far.

For ideas, consult the chapters 'Keeping Your Characters and Your Love Scenes Chaste' and 'Building Erotic Tension Without Erotic Action'. You can describe the girl's yearning fantasies about a tight embrace with the boy of her desire, as well as the electric tingle when his fingers brush her arm for the first time. The first kiss can be a major plot event, and the chapter 'The Couple's First Kiss' offers suggestions.

CHILDREN'S FICTION

If the main characters in a children's book are adults – a prince and a princess, for example – their love scene is characterised by kindness and courtesy.

If the main characters are children, they may passively witness or be actively involved in a love scene between adults – for example, when their single dad falls in love. Keep such love scenes simple, at a level the child can understand, and focus on getting the new character's personality across.

Sex, whether graphic or implied, doesn't belong in a children's book.

HISTORICAL FICTION

The challenge in writing love scenes for Historical fiction lies in balancing authentic historical attitudes with modern sensitivities. What was considered proper or noble in that period may now be considered awkward or offensive. If your characters act like modern people, the story loses its authenticity, but if they behave like people of their time, readers may despise them. Try to find a compromise that works for your story, the characters and the scene.

Be careful about erotic action. Sex outside marriage had different meanings, implications and consequences than today. If the characters have sex, they are aware of what they sacrifice or risk – and the reader needs to be aware of this too. Keeping the characters chaste, so they save themselves for marriage is probably the safest option for them and your novel. But of course, your plot may demand otherwise.

You may these chapters useful: 'Keeping Your Characters and Your Love Scenes Chaste', 'Building Erotic Tension Without Erotic Action', as well as the historical note in the chapter 'Clothing – And How To Remove It'.

INSPIRATIONAL FICTION

In this kind of story, the main characters serve as role models. They seek to do the right thing (although they don't always succeed), upholding their values and the rules of their faith.

This affects how they act in love scenes. They won't say 'I love you,' until they are willing to commit to a relationship. They won't engage in spontaneous sex, but instead keep themselves pure for marriage. The chapter 'Keeping Your Characters and Your Love Scenes Chaste' will be helpful for this.

However, they may be tempted. For this, you can create erotic tension. Show how the characters resist the temptation to protect both themselves and the loved one. Study the chapter 'Building Erotic Tension Without Erotic Action' to get the nuances right.

CHAPTER 34

DIFFERENT ROMANCE SUBGENRES

Susanne McCarthy

Romance is still by far the most popular fiction genre, and inevitably there are numerous subgenres within the category. These can be defined by where they sit on the spectrum of erotic content.

INSPIRATIONAL ROMANCE

Moral or religious ethics usually predominate in the plot, and may create the conflict which keeps the couple apart. The relationship between them is likely to be warmer than in other genres, with less of the argumentative banter – the conflict element is more likely to be tinged with regret.

They may experience temptation, but they resist it until they are sure they are committed to the relationship. This holding back means that many of your love scenes will be built around fleeting glances, the occasional passing touch of a hand – even the smallest contact holds a lot of significance. When they finally kiss, it is tender and loving.

You may find useful pointers in the chapters 'Keeping Your Characters and Your Love Scenes Chaste' and 'The Couple's First Kiss'.

YOUNG ADULT ROMANCE

These are often about first love, or a first love arises within the plot, which will often be an adventure. The protagonists are younger – often teenagers – so have little or no experience other than the odd kiss behind the bike sheds. This lack of experience may lead to misunderstandings when romantic approaches are made inappropriately, or not made when hoped for.

Any approach to kissing or more is very tentative and probably a bit clumsy. They may be curious about love-making, and may fantasise a lot (though probably rather innocently) but if you want to go further, do it with care!

Look at the chapters 'Keeping Your Characters and Your Love Scenes Chaste' and 'The Couple's First Kiss'.

SWEET ROMANCE
(also called 'Traditional Romance' or 'Heart-Warming Romance)

These may have a historical or contemporary setting. The partners are adults, but typically the female partner has limited romantic experience – though in other areas of her life she may well be feisty, confident, successful.

The attraction between them is strong, but with more emphasis on character than sexual attraction. The romantic relationship is likely to develop quite slowly as conflicts and misunderstandings are resolved, but there are longing thoughts and some fantasising. Actual physical contact is likely to only come towards the end. There are kisses – often very passionate – and there may be some erotic touch and responses, though clothing gets usually only slightly disarranged rather than removed.

There is always a Happy-Ever-After, and around the point where this is confirmed your couple may make love. But the bedroom door remains discreetly closed – though you can have the morning after.

The chapters 'Keeping Your Characters and Your Love Scenes Chaste', 'The Couple's First Kiss' and 'Keeping the Bedroom Door Closed – How To Imply Intimacy Without Showing It' contain useful pointers.

MAINSTREAM ROMANCE

These novels may have a historical or contemporary setting. You can have any type of characters, but there is a strong sexual attraction between them from the start – and an equally strong conflict keeping them apart.

The story takes you through the whole journey from their first meeting, their resistance to the attraction between them, the temptations and moments of surrender followed by fiercer resistance, to the key turning point when all the conflicts are brought out into the open and finally resolved, and we reach the Happy-Ever-After.

Hence there are numerous love scenes throughout – from their initial contact and feelings of attraction/resistance, lots of fantasising (often quite erotic) kissing and touching, escalating through the story. But this is balanced by the development of the relationship between the lovers as they get to know each other and the misunderstandings are worked out.

There is often only one scene of erotic action, towards the end of the story – often just before the point of conflict resolution. But this is not a fixed rule – there may be several scenes, and one may come early in the story (especially in a 'secret baby' story.)

The language used is not explicit, though the scenes of love-making can be very explicit (see the chapter 'How to Write Erotic Scenes'). These scenes can be fierce or tender, but will be clearly consensual (even in a 'coerced marriage' story.) There may well be some variety – implicit or explicit – including the acts described in the chapter on 'Getting Seriously Intimate'. There may also be some mild sex-play – blindfolding, a little light bondage – but probably not spanking.

EROTIC ROMANCE

There is a lot of erotic action from the beginning, but there is also a plot with a strong love story. The woman is a very active partner, and may well instigate the sex. There is variety, sex-play, and the language may be explicit (the male and female 'c' words, for example.)

And gradually they each begin to realise that they want more from this relationship than 'just sex'. You can feed this into your love scenes, which gradually change in flavour. They may be wary of speaking about their feelings, as that wasn't on the agenda when the relationship began. But at last, as with a mainstream romance, they reach a crisis point when they realise that must resolve the issue or lose the relationship, and one of them takes the risk of saying "I love you."

EROTICA AND BDSM

There is usually very little plot or romance – it's all about the sex, in all its wild varieties. The focus of love scenes is on erotic tension and intimate action rather than emotion. If you are planning to write in these genres, you probably don't need any guidance from us. Just a brief but important reminder – the BDSM (bondage, domination, sadism, masochism) community in particular are very insistent on explicit consent.

OTHER ROMANCE SUBGENRES

You may encounter many more subgenres from Paranormal Romance to Romantic Suspense, from Historical Romance to Science Fiction Romance. New subgenres are created and labelled all the time, and if they're trending in a big way, they get divided into sub-subgenres and even sub-sub-subgenres.

For example, Historical Romance is a subgenre of Romance, and its sub-subgenres span Mediaeval Romance, Regency Romance, Victorian Romance and more. Each of those may then be divided further, so you get labels like Medieval Time Travel Romance, Regency Mystery Romance, and Victorian Paranormal Romance.

Don't let this profusion of categories confuse you. They're simply labels to help publishers, booksellers and readers know instantly what's inside. They're also useful for talking shop with literary agents and fellow writers.

There isn't a single definitive taxonomy for Romance subgenres. You'll find that Amazon uses a different system than Barnes & Noble, and the bookshop chains in your country, the big book fairs and the Romance authors' associations use yet other categories.

Towards the end of the 20th century, genres and subgenres were rigid. Each book was expected to belong to just one specific category, and authors were constrained to write exactly what was expected in that subgenre. For example, Regency Romance had to be a clean read without erotic tension or intimate action. Now in the 21st century, genre definitions and contents are far more fluid, and many books spread across several genres anyway.

Excerpt from *Chasing Stars*
by Susanne McCarthy

This is how I have used some of the techniques described in this book. The setting is Javier's fabulous yacht, cruising the Mediterranean.

As you study this excerpt, observe the techniques I applied.

- Placing the scene: the erotic tension has been building up for a couple of weeks, now is the right time for it to explode.

- Conflict: Kat has a secret – she hasn't told Javier why she is on the yacht. The reasons behind it mean that she feels guilty about being with him, and knows she must leave in three days when they dock in Antibes.

- Using different senses: the scent of his skin, the feel of the satin coverlet beneath her, the warm glow of the bedside light.

- Clothes – particularly her thoughts about her underwear!

- Dialogue is sprinkled into the scene, and touches of humour.

- Look at how I have mingled action with reaction, for example when he caresses her breasts.

- Note the brief reference to her previous experience – it adds just a little to the way she is experiencing this.

- The naming of parts – look at the language I have used. And the way I avoided naming or describing his endowments: *He was wearing navy blue silk jersey jockey shorts, clinging against his narrow hips and... She had forgotten to breathe again...*

- Consent – this is very clear from her whispered "please" and the way she moves invitingly.

Now read:

"I... I was just thinking... It's getting late. I ought to be going."

"You don't have to."

Her breath hitched in her throat. His dark eyes held a question – she knew the answer should be no, but the hunger inside her was stronger than caution, stronger than guilt.

As he came round the table towards her she felt as if she was caught in a spell. The rational part of her mind was clanging with alarm bells – this was wrong, wrong, wrong. But she didn't want to be right. The wicked voice of temptation was whispering inside her head; *Only three days. Why not?*

He took her hand, raising it to his lips and placing a feather-light kiss on the racing pulse inside her wrist. His voice was a husky promise. "Stay here. Stay the night."

Just the way he was looking at her was melting her inside. Those eyes... so dark... dark as sin... He drew her to her feet, still holding her hand – she knew she could escape if she wanted to. But she didn't want to.

"You're beautiful," he murmured. "I don't think you know how beautiful you are."

She laughed a little unsteadily. "I think you must have had too much wine."

He shook his head. "Not at all. Your skin is like cream silk, you have the grace of a dancer. And your hair – it's just glorious. The colour of vine-leaves in autumn." He ran his fingers into it, drawing it all to the back of her head, so that she was held prisoner, gazing up into the drowning pools of his eyes.

It would be so good to believe he meant it… *Stop thinking… Just enjoy the moment…* The temptation was aching inside her. And after all, they would be back in Antibes in a couple of days…

Some reckless spirit had caught hold of her. She may be about to make the biggest mistake of her life, but she didn't care. And as his mouth came down on hers, the last traces of her resistance seemed to evaporate. She had no defences left.

All her senses were focused on this moment – with every breath, the subtle musky scent of his skin was intoxicating her, silencing the whispering voice of sanity. His lips were warm and firm, coaxing hers apart; his hot tongue slipped inside, swirling over all the sensitive membranes, seeking all the deep secret corners within.

He was luring her into a magical world of desire, his kiss tender and enticing. With no conscious thought she had lifted her arms to wrap them around his neck, curving her supple body against his, conveying a message he would not mistake.

His marauding hand had slipped beneath her T-shirt, stroking up over her smooth skin, finding the warm, round swell of her breast. A soft moan escaped her throat as his thumb brushed over the taut, tender nub of her nipple, stirring some ancient instinct, as old as Eve, urging her to surrender.

"Will you stay?" he whispered, huskily soft against her ear.

She closed her eyes, knowing there was only one answer. "Yes…"

With one easy movement he scooped her up in his arms and carried her inside, carried her to the bed.

She closed her eyes, stretching like a cat on the silken coverlet. His weight came down beside her, and he drew her close against him again, his mouth closing over hers in a deep, sensuous kiss. She could only surrender, everything feminine inside her responding to his urgent male demand.

His tongue was swirling deep into her mouth, exploring all the most secret, sensitive places. His hand stroked down her spine and over the smooth swell of her bottom, drawing her closer, making her devastatingly aware of the hard tension of his male arousal.

A small whimper of protest broke from her throat as his lips finally left hers, but it was only to dust scalding kisses over her trembling eyelids and her delicate temple, where a racing pulse beat beneath her skin. Her breathing was ragged, her blood racing in her veins as if she had a fever.

With a subtle movement he eased his fingers beneath her work T-shirt, and a small sigh escaped her throat as she felt his fingers brush against the underside of her breast. The pad of his thumb was teasing at the tender bud of her nipple, stirring a shimmering response inside her.

He grunted his approval as she tugged the T-shirt off impatiently over her head. Damn cheap and sensible cotton underwear, she reflected fleetingly – why couldn't she be wearing something lacy and seductive?

Not that he seemed to notice. With a deftness she didn't care to dwell on, he unhooked her bra with one hand and tossed it aside.

"Did I mention that you have all the essential curves, in exactly the right proportions?" he growled thickly, his hot gaze lingering over the ripe swell of her naked breasts, creamy pale against the slightly richer cream where the sun had kissed her.

She gurgled with laughter. "They're not very big."

"Who needs big?" he argued. "These fit very nicely." He demonstrated by encompassing the whole swell of her breast in one hand, moulding it with his long, strong fingers. "You see?"

She felt the sensitive peak tauten, crushing itself into his palm.

His mouth claimed hers again, drugging her senses. She closed her eyes, letting her hands slide into his hair as their tongues swirled together. She was lost in a kiss that seemed to last a million years – if this was crazy, she no longer wanted to be sane.

This was the only reality, this warm cocoon of pure sensation – his hot mouth on hers, his moist, sinuous tongue invading every deep corner, the feel of satin beneath her, and the warm glow of the light beside the bed bathing them both in gold.

She felt her blood heat to fever pitch as his kisses trailed down the long curve of her throat to find the sensitive spot in the hollow of her shoulder – hot, open-mouthed kisses against her smooth skin, scorching a path over the aching curve of her breasts as she gasped in pleasure, writhing beneath his touch.

The pink buds of her nipples were taut with anticipation as he circled tantalisingly closer, until at last his mouth closed over one exquisitely sensitised peak, grazing it lightly with his hard white teeth, lapping and swirling over it with his hot, moist tongue, suckling it with a deep, sweet rhythm that sizzled along her nerve fibres to pierce her brain.

When he drew back she almost sobbed in frustration, but it was only to unbutton his shirt. She watched from beneath her lashes as he shrugged it aside. She had seen his body before, of course – yesterday, down on the beach. But the sheer male beauty of that sun-bronzed, hard-muscled torso still took her breath away.

His hand dropped to the waistband of his dark grey cotton chinos, unfastening the button and... phew... sliding down the zip. She sucked in a desperate gasp of air, closing her eyes but then opening them again – she didn't want to miss this.

He was wearing navy blue silk jersey jockey shorts, clinging against his narrow hips and...

She had forgotten to breathe again…

He moved back to the bed, kneeling across her thighs, trapping her half-naked beneath him. His eyes were lit with a hot flame of desire, scorching her creamy skin as he surveyed the territory laid out for his appreciation. She lifted her arms back above her head, wriggling in eager invitation.

"If you keep doing that," he growled darkly, "you're likely to find things move a great deal too quickly."

She laughed, emboldened by the adrenalin racing through her bloodstream. "Maybe I like the sound of that."

"Minx." He hooked one fingertip into the waistband of her shorts. "Maybe you should take these off?" he suggested.

Her heart thudded – she should have known he would call her on that one. But some wicked demon inside her prompted her to respond with a provocative smile, and her hand went to the button at the side of her waistband.

Unfortunately her clumsy fingers rather undermined her attempt to appear cool, as if making love with a gorgeous hunk of male was no big deal for her.

Actually it was her first time – well, her first time with a gorgeous hunk, anyway. One nice-but-dull and one persistent-for-a-whole-month-then-vanished-into-the-mist-after-two-weeks didn't really add up to much in the way of experience.

But every girl deserved a treat – and a bruised heart and a guilty conscience were a small price to pay.

"Let me," he offered, his velvet voice straight out of her steamiest fantasy.

He dealt with the impediment in seconds, then he was drawing the shorts down slowly over her slim hips, inch by inch, that beguiling smile teasing her with unspoken promises.

He hooked her knickers as he went, and she lifted her hips to let them pass as he stripped them from her, whipping them down to her ankles and tossing them aside, leaving her naked on the bed.

"I'm not sure if I mentioned this before," he remarked as if making polite conversation, "but your legs were the first thing I noticed about you. They are the most fabulous pair of legs I've ever seen. They start down here…" He picked up one foot, and placed a kiss just below her ankle. "And go all the way up…" He was tracing a hot path of kisses up her calf, past her knee. "To here…" He continued working his way up the inner side of her thigh. "To here…"

Her breath caught in her throat as he reached very top.

"And by the way, I'm so glad you don't go the full Brazilian," he added as he teased his fingers through the crown of russet curls that concealed her most secret places. "I like a little… decoration."

She gurgled with laughter, but then uttered a small gasp as she felt the heat of his breath against her most sensitive hidden membranes.

His tongue lapped in, finding the tiny seed-pearl nestled within the folds of crimson velvet, the focus of all her nerve-fibres. Her response ignited, her spine curling as an exquisite sting of pleasure rippled through her.

She was being swept away in a warm tide of sensuality that was melting her bones to honey. A languid sigh purred from her lips as he moved to lie above her, the powerful muscles in his shoulders bunched as he held his weight from crushing her. For one endless moment the universe seemed to stand still.

"Please…" she whispered, her thighs parting invitingly to surrender her feminine core to the hard thrust of his possession.

She opened her eyes to gaze up at him as they moved to the sensual rhythm he dictated – slowly at first, and then quickening as some elemental force seemed to take control of them both, driving them relentlessly, fast and wild, like tongues of flame dancing together, hotter than the heart of the sun.

She felt as if she was soaring, upward and upward to dizzying heights, the tension coiling inside her, her breathing ragged as her heartbeat raced out of control.

And then a last wild tremor ripped through her, and the cry she heard was her own as she tipped over the edge to fall, tumbling through air, to land in his arms on the wide bed.

Excerpt from *Storm Dancer*
by Rayne Hall

Storm Dancer is a dark-epic fantasy novel. The first meeting between the two characters occurs several chapters into the book, so the reader already knows them, their personalities, their backstories and their goals.

Merida is a magician, honest, fastidious, resourceful and prudish. On assignment in a foreign country, she was captured by the ruler and imprisoned in his harem. She managed to escape by posing as a whiteseer, a kind of fortune-teller who keeps her face, body and hair covered in white clay. On no account will she allow the Consort's greenbelts to capture her again.

Dahoud is a warrior with a dark secret. He yearns to protect women... but he is possessed by a demon that drives him to subdue women with force. Whenever Dahoud feels attraction for a woman, the Djinn manipulates his mind to use violence. As an honourable man, Dahoud seeks to protect women from the evil inside him. Dahoud is strongly attracted to bellydancers and female fighters, and he dreams of rescuing a woman in distress. His assignment: to capture a runaway concubine and return her to the Consort.

As you read this excerpt, pay attention to the following:

- This is an example of the 'First Meeting in Disguise' scenario, because Merida disguises herself first as a whiteseer and then as a bellydancer. Observe how he reacts to her based on what he believes she is

- Observe how Merida consciously reacts to Dahoud's role (greenbelt), even while her subconscious perceives him as a special individual

- Merida and Dahoud are strongly attracted to each other, but both fight against the attraction. Merida suppresses all thought of attraction because he's the enemy, and because of her own prudish nature. Dahoud suppresses his attraction because it would unleash the djinn

- In the section starting with 'Suddenly, the air sang with tension...' notice how I slowed down the moment of their first encounter to build tension and how I used sensory impressions to draw attention to the experience

- In the section starting 'One-two-three, one-two-three...' notice how Merida becomes aware of Dahoud's attention (and how it makes her feel)

- See how I changed the Point-of-View from Merida's perspective to Dahoud's at the chapter break

- The readers already know that Dahoud is attracted to dancers and to women who can fight, and that he has a fantasy of protecting a woman in distress. When these three factors combine, they resonate with the readers as strongly as with Dahoud himself

- I created erotic tension in the chapter from Dahoud's PoV by making him very aware of Merida sexually, at the same time compelling him to suppress any erotic thoughts.

Merida strode along the riverbank until she found a willow-shaded section abundant with abundant white clay. Here she could fill her jar and renew her body paint. The substance slid silky-soft and cool between her fingers. It felt so good that she slapped it on by the handful, and finally burrowed herself in the silky mud. This place was rich in magic energy. For a long time, Merida lay on her back, with her limbs spread and her eyes closed, to absorb the earth's blessing and listen to the river sucking softly at the banks. She drifted into healing, blissful sleep.

A horse's neigh, followed by excited giggles, jolted her awake. A small crowd had gathered on the riverbank to stare at the sleeping seer.

She jumped up, pulled her hair forward over her chest lest any female forms should be visible under the still-damp fabric, and clambered up with as much dignity as she could muster.

"A reading, a reading! Seer, a reading!" a dozen voices clamoured at once. She obliged with recommendations for a virtuous lifestyle, and collected copper rings in her pouch.

Suddenly the air sang with danger. A rider vaulted off his grey horse. The sight of his moss-green tunic and plaited belt hit her guts. This was one of the Consort's henchmen, a thousand miles from the palace. Had he come to arrest her?

She took a step back, poised for flight.

"A reading, please, seer." His voice was deep like a slow-flowing river, smooth on top but dangerous beneath.

She allowed herself to meet his eyes, as if she had nothing to fear from his kind. Although his mouth smiled, his eyes were bitter-dark like olives. An aura of vibrant intelligence was enveloped in intense bitterness, and under his cheerful courtesy, pain radiated from him like heat searing from a fire.

Her instincts screamed at her to pull free from the dangerous power before it could burn her, but a genuine wandering seer would not panic at the sight of a palace official, and bolting would draw his suspicion.

She forced herself to stay in her role. "Your hands," she demanded, careful to hide her accent.

The hands were wrong. Brown, with short dirty nails, calloused, rough and ridged with old scars, they did not belong to a courtier, nor even to a guard.

At the moment of touch, shock surged through her, sending tingles all over her body. Her stomach felt as if a pestle was running along the inside of a stone mortar. Several futures flashed by her vision, too fast to hold, then his past dragged her in. She heard screams of terror and pain, and smelled the stench of scorching flesh. This man was burning in the fire of his own soul.

Gasping for breath, she jerked away. "I can't… your past…"

His hands clasped around her wrists. "I'm sorry you had to see that, but please look beyond it if you can."

"I can't advise you on a problem of that magnitude." She tried to pull free from his crushing grip.

"I'm not asking about that. I want advice for a current mission." He lowered his voice to a confidential whisper. "I'm looking for a concubine escaped from the royal harem. A colleague of yours told me I might find her here."

She forced slow breath into her lungs to slow her thudding heart. Shutting out the danger tinglings as best she could, she rubbed the man's palms, traced the lines with her nails, sniffed at the fingers. They smelled of leather and horse.

Caution prodded her to send him on a false path, preferably back to distant Quislabat, but Honesty would not permit her to speak a lie, not even to a despicable greenbelt, not even to protect herself. Instinct warred with honour like two cubs tearing the same piece of flesh. She searched for a sentence that contained the truth he sought, without exposing herself to danger.

Finally, she said, "Don't underestimate that missing person," and dropped his hands.

When his brows tightened in a frown, as if he was about to ask for clarification, she raised her chin haughtily in the whiteseer manner. "Next."

"Thank you, seer." He pressed a copper ring into her palm and mounted his horse.

Merida scanned an old woman's hand, but from the corner of her eye she watched until she was certain the silver horse and green tunic had vanished in the distance.

She finished the fifth reading and placed the grateful client's payment in her pouch when a girl of Kadiffe's age planted herself squarely before her. "Why you be readin' today? It be the solstice."

Scarf-wrapped heads exchanged bewildered glances. Voices, laced with suspicion, muttered about 'solstice' and 'seclusion'.

"The solstice?" she repeated brightly. "Of course. How could I forget the seclusion! I'd better not do any more readings today. Thank you, good people." Cursing her ignorance about seers' customs, she strode off with enforced calm.

Before long, the greenbelt would realise the seer had worked on a forbidden day, concluding she was a fake. If he found her, her freedom was forfeit. She must not stay in seer disguise a moment longer.

Out of sight of her erstwhile clients, she immersed herself in the river. The water carried away the clay, and the dress dried quickly in the searing sun, but she was still wearing a white dress, and her long copper-coloured hair was conspicuous.

She needed a new disguise.

*

Djildit Town smelled worse than a cattle pen. Crippled beggars wailed their pleas while tavern-keepers accosted passers-by with promises of jugglers, dancers and storytelling acrobats. Crudely painted signs advertised bellydancers, tattooed maidens and women with two heads. Vending stalls with copper pots and earthenware crowded the narrow alleys, and Merida dodged bickering shoppers, donkeys and sheep.

The town's broadest road led to a heavily guarded bridge across the river. Beyond that lay the country of Zigazia, blue in the heat-mist. The uniformed men at this border took their duty seriously, checking passes, interrogating and body-searching everyone leaving the Queendom. Merida still had no pass. What now?

Evening sun slanted from the rooftops. Daytime was running out. Merida returned to the warren of alleys where she tried to blend into the crowd of shoppers, but among the yellow and orange garments, her white dress stood out. She fingered the coppers in her pouch. Five tanni might buy a decent headscarf, but no dress. No longer a whiteseer, she did not even have the means to earn more.

"Look at my lovely clothes," a rag-seller trilled. "Lovely, lush, luxurious! Anything from this stall for just one tanni."

The thought of wearing someone else's cast-offs was revolting, but it was the only way to change her appearance fast. Merida dipped her hands into the heap of garish fabrics. "Have these been laundered properly?"

"My clothes are very clean," the woman assured her. "I wash them myself. Lovely, lush things they are. Buy two, get the third one free."

Merida knelt on the packed dirt, next to two bony cats sunning themselves in a patch of receding light, and rummaged through the baskets. She found only one tunic, much too short for her, with the underarm seams split and the hem frayed, as red as the sinking sun, the most sinful of colours. But even now, the greenbelt might be scanning the streets, asking questions about a woman in white.

Already, the sun was vanishing behind the houses, the shutters of shops clattered shut, and vendors rolled up the awnings of their stalls. With a pointed glance at her indecisive customer, the rag-seller started to stuff her wares into baskets.

Merida grabbed the tunic and added two garish shawls with unravelling tassels. She tossed two coppers on the table, and changed behind the stall's curtain. The tunic was not only too short, but too low at the front, showing almost a whole finger-breath of Merida's breasts. She draped the yellow scarf to hide the cleavage. Her arms and calves remained bare, and she could not even cover them with clay. She felt very sinful.

A uniformed watchman prodded a beggar with his spear. "No loitering in this town at night."

Merida marched fast, pretending to have a purpose. Darkness fell fast, and nothing remained of the day except lingering heat.

The inn near the bridge had a huge canine painted on its façade, next to a sign promising *Darrian Dansers Evry Night. Eksotig and Apsollutly Gennwin,* complete with a drawing of a female torso with unrealistic curves. The clacking steps of spear-armed guards drove Merida into the inn's courtyard where camels slurped from a trough. A smell of jasmine was even stronger than the reek of animal sweat and dung. Torches waved their yellow flames in the descending gloom.

Several people argued in the doorway. "Promising dancers you don't have," an old man grumbled. "I call that cheating. I'll complain to the authorities."

"Please," a black-haired man with drooping cheeks beseeched him. "We be havin' full music tonight, and dancers be back tomorrow."

The woman pulled her husband by the arm. "There are other shows in town. Let's enjoy the rest of the night and see the woman with two heads. Tomorrow we'll complain to the authorities."

Merida waited until the incensed customers had left, and addressed the drooping-cheeked man. "Excuse me. Are you the landlord of this establishment? What are the prices for one night's accommodation?"

He eyed her up and down, and obviously judged her to be of an unlucrative client class. "Six tanni for a place on the roof."

She had three tanni left and nowhere else to go. "I'm afraid -"

"You be wantin' a place, or not?" he barked through big pointed teeth. His drooping cheeks wobbled. It was easy to see how the Black Dog Inn had gained its name. "The roof be getting' full fast. Pay now, you be squeezin' in."

"Squeezing in?" she repeated feebly. That sounded worse than a dormitory. Maybe there were even men sleeping on that roof.

Another cluster of patrons left, grumbling about the cancelled entertainment. The Black Dog wrung his hands, entreating them in vain to stay.

An idea shot into Merida's head. "Are you seeking to hire a performer for tonight? I'm an accomplished dancer with lots of experience. From Darria." A lie. A shameful, sinful lie. She would have to atone for it later. For now, she trusted he would not guess her foreign accent's real origin. The dancer at the palace had earned thirty tanni. Provincial prices would be lower. "Fifteen tanni."

"You be gettin' no tanni from me." He shimmied his shoulders. "Wobblin' titties, like. Gettin' tips." His gaze travelled down the front of her dress. "Where be your costume?"

She plastered her most charming smile to her face, unwrapped the yellow scarf from her chest and knotted it around her lower torso. "Will this do?"

When he gazed at her cleavage, a hot flush burnt her face. Now she had added gross indecency to her list of sins. Once she got back to Riverland, she would have to do heavy penance to purify her soul.

She flicked four technically refined hip-drops. "I want a meal and accommodation for the night."

"Very fine." His lips pursed in contemplation of the exposed cleavage. "You be getting' food leftovers from the kitchen, and a space on the roof."

"I'll eat leftovers, but I insist on a private room."

His lips widened. "Private room, yes. Very private. First, you be dancin'. Be quick."

A drum started to throb, and a harp's strings silvered the air.

Without light or a mirror, Merida used the stolen black face-paint to draw a hasty rim around her eyes. Recalling everything the teacher had told the concubines about tavern dancing, she hurried to make her entrance. If only she had finger cymbals or a tambourine!

The torch-lit dining room smelled of coriander and roasted flesh. With a confident pose copied from the palace dancer, Merida floated into the river of welcoming applause.

The drum delivered a clear rhythm: *Doum tek, doumdoum tek, doum-tek, doumdoum-tek.*

Four steps forward, eight to the left, eight to the right... Not enough space between the benches. Hipdrops, hiplifts, shimmied circles.

The rhythm switched to the Darrian six-count: *Doum-doum-doum doum-doum doum.* As a supposed Darrian, she had to cope. Three-step shuffle left, three-step shuffle right. When the women at the table clapped, her feet slid into the pattern, and the joy of music and movement seeped into her limbs. This was supposed to be work. Was she permitted to feel pleasure?

When she added the Darrian neck-slides Haurvatat had taught her, women, rather than men, cheered her on, yelping and ululating with pleasure. These were respectable-looking tradeswomen in almost decent clothes, so perhaps bellydancing was not an entirely sinful act. Merida absorbed their response and converted it to magical power. Soon she was rising inside a cloud of a happy trance.

She remembered to keep her hands near her throat to hide her cleavage, but it seemed the custom to drop coppers down her front. Fortunately, it was only the women who did it. The cool rings slid down between her breasts and jingled below her waist.

One-two-three, one-two-three.... Merida danced happily towards the far end of the room, giving the people at every table a sincere beaming smile. The final corner was almost dark, and she launched into a full-body shimmy before she saw the man's face. The greenbelt.

He was not wearing the turban, and his green tunic looked grey in the dim light, but it was him, and his eyes grazed her with hunger. Did he admire her dance, did he desire her body, or did he suspect who she was? The drum of fear beat in her chest.

Wanting to bolt, Merida forced herself to keep dancing. He stood, holding up a copper ring in one hand and beckoning her close with the other. Before he could drop his tanni down her front, Merida fled to the safety of the friendly tradeswomen.

Shutting out the greenbelt's presence and assuring herself that he could not possibly guess her identity, she danced until the musicians put their instruments down.

In the kitchen, she asked for a jug of water and the promised meal. A gruff female cook pushed a bowl into her hands, the kind of dish dogs in Riverland ate from. Gristly bones stuck out of the grey mush, and a chunk of yam showed bite marks. These were not remnants from the cooking pots, but what the patrons had left on their plates.

"Would you show me to my room, please?"

The cook squinted. "Your room?"

"Black Dog... I mean, the landlord, promised me a private room for tonight."

The woman jerked her head at the staircase. "Up there, corridor to the left, the door at the end."

The tradeswomen, chattering in good spirits, were withdrawing for the night. They had expensive rooms in the right wing, with real wooden doors.

The allocated chamber was windowless and exuded sticky wheat moon heat, and had not been cleaned or tidied since its previous occupation. Merida told herself she could not expect Riverian standards here. At least she had a room to herself, with a heavy curtain over the entrance, which was better than sharing roof-space with strange men.

She gulped down half the water. She stirred the greasy goo in search of non-animal matter and contemplated scraping the meat juice off a carrot slice, but put it down uneaten.

After piling the earned copper rings next to the sleeping mat, she cheered. Thirty-two tanni would buy the provisions she needed for the journey into Zigazia. She pulled off the sweat-heavy tunic. Since the water was too sparse for a proper wash, she rubbed it over her body. Tomorrow, she would buy a new dress, and then she would never again put on clothes someone else had worn.

"Fine, fine," said a man's voice from the door curtain. "I be comin' to you now."

Merida snatched up the yellow scarf and held it before her naked front. "Get out!"

Black Dog's drooping cheeks quivered with excitement. "Titties-wobblin' for me now."

His arms opened to embrace her.

"Get out!" she yelled again, backing towards the wall.

When his hands grabbed her shoulders, her body locked rigid. This could not be happening. Not to her.

His tongue slid across his lips like a fat pink slug. His fingers worked under the fabric and cupped her breast. Merida snapped out of her trance.

She stomped down hard on his foot, rammed a knee into his groin and punched the Woodpecker sequence into his face. She followed it with The Boar's Tusk and an extra-fast Thunder Cloud.

When he sagged to the ground, she applied The Toad's Vengeance. For good measure, she smashed the jug over his skull and slammed the food bowl, upside down, into his face. His grunts turned to groans. Since he lay curled with his hands guarding the crotch, she stomped him into the kidneys. This was a forbidden move that would get her expelled from the Disciplined Path class, but nobody would find out. She kicked once more. Symmetry mattered.

She fled from the room, seeking safety. But where? Not in the streets of the night, nor among the rabble on the roof.

The nice tradeswomen had rooms in the other wing. Tying the scarf around her torso, Merida raced down the dark corridor.

She banged at the first wooden door. It opened at once.

A male chest. Unclothed. Further down... She gulped. He was not wearing any garment at all.

Footsteps pounded the corridor. "I be getting' you, you bitch!" Black Dog panted. "You be payin' for this." She had not hit her assailant hard enough, and now he was after her. Panic threatened to throttle her.

Black Dog was a proven danger. The man at the door might be safe.

"Please, good sir, help me! I need your protection."

"Come in."

Once in the room, the door snapped shut behind her, and a bolt slammed.

To avoid seeing her rescuer's unclothed body in the sparse light of the oil-lamp, she looked at his face.

The greenbelt.

[Chapter break]

Dahoud stared. The woman in his bedroom wore a big turban, a scarf clutched to her chest, and nothing else. She was tall, fair-skinned, flushed and frightened. Her eyes darted as if looking for an escape route.

He cleared his throat.

Someone else pounded at the door with the ferocity of a battering ram. "Open up!"

Dahoud could not hope this surprise visitor would be as delightful as the one already in his room. He pulled the door open. "What do you want?"

The landlord's face glowered, caked with blood and blooming with bruises. A swollen lump rose under his eye. "I be wantin' that dancer."

"Too late. I be wantin' her myself." Dahoud slammed the door shut and bolted it. "Did you do that to his face?"

"In self-defence. If you lay a finger on me, I'll do the same to you."

A woman who could fight! His body pulsed with excitement. It would be delicious to measure her strength.

Her fingers pulled at the scarf, as if trying to make the fabric stretch it to cover more skin. She was as skittish as a frightened horse.

He picked up his under-tunic from the floor and tossed it to her. "Wear this."

When she held it to her nose and sniffed at it, he was glad it was clean. He had only worn it four days.

He turned to the window to let her dress. Since his own nudity might make her nervous, he slipped the green tunic on and fastened the plaited belt around it.

In the meantime, she had draped the shawl over the under-tunic, hiding every hint of breast. "Thank you, kind sir." She tiptoed towards the door. "I'll return the garment as soon as I have the means."

A wave of warmth washed through him and pounded him with urgency. "Wait! Do you have somewhere to go? Stay here. I'll pay your fee for a night."

"I'm no whore!" Her words lashed across his face.

His face fired. He had said the wrong thing. "I just… I want you to be safe for tonight. You take the mat. I'll sleep on the floor." For once in his life, he had the chance to redeem himself. He would shelter this woman chastely from harm. Yearning need twisted through his chest. "I won't touch you, I promise."

Hesitation flickered over her face, and her glance darted between the window and the door.

He unsheathed his sword and held it out to her, hilt first. The curved blade was the only item he kept from his legion days. "Will this make you feel better?"

She did not touch the weapon, but the tension dripped from her shoulders. "I'll be glad to stay the night. Thank you, sir."

Like a traveller who sees the oasis after a long desert journey, Dahoud thanked the Mighty Ones for their gift. Tonight he would complete his defeat of the djinn.

He pushed the sword back into its sheath. "I'm Dahoud. What's your name?"

"M... My name is Zaina." She blushed as she spoke.

A Darrian name. "Sleep well, Zaina," he said in her native tongue. "Tomorrow we'll plan how to keep you safe."

"Yes, sir. Thank you, sir."

Joy sang like wine in his blood. He savoured the precious, poignant pleasure of the moment.

As she curled into a tight ball on the mat, his thoughts circled around her like a hawk above prey. Other bellydancers floated in the music and shared their joy with the audience, but Zaina's dance had had the dogged determination of a legion drill. Was she new to her art? Why did a grown woman take up tavern dancing as a new career? What had she done before, and what fate had forced her on this new path? Why did she keep her turban on to sleep? Other dancers liked to toss their hair, but she kept hers hidden. Had she shaved her skull to rid it of lice, or had it been cropped to punish a prostitute? How good a fighter was she? How long would she last against Dahoud?

He pushed the wrestling out of his mind before it could kindle and set his fantasies on fire, and planned how he would capture the fake whiteseer.

*

When the morning sun poured through the window, golden and clear, Dahoud woke with a light heart. He had not touched the dancer. Faced with temptation, he had stayed strong. His control of the djinn was complete.

"Good morning, Zaina. Will you join me for breakfast?"

She stretched, yawned, and adjusted her sleep-dislodged turban. As she fumbled with the cloth, a thick mane of copper hair spilled over her shoulders. Bronze! Recall shot through him like a dart: the Riverian magician had tossed such hair.

Zaina was the rain dancer, the fake seer, the runaway concubine.

He acted at once. He grabbed her from behind, locked his hands under her ribcage and forced the air from her lungs.

"Don't hurt me," she whimpered. As soon as he relaxed his grip, her elbow rammed into his stomach. Fists rained into his face and slammed on his skull.

A heartbeat later, she unbolted the door and vanished. He fastened his dagger belt and vaulted out of the window.

She was racing out of the courtyard into the road, glancing over her shoulder, bumping through market stalls. She knocked over a display of copper pots. The vessels clattered onto the road and forced him to slow.

"Rapist! Rapist!" she yelled, running.

How dare she! He would get her.

"Stop the mangy greenbelt!" a dozen voices screeched. "Save the girl!"

People crowded in on him. A black-clad giant blocked his path. Something slammed on his head. The world turned orange, then black.

DEAR READER,

I hope you found these tips helpful and will apply them to give your love scenes the emotional power your story deserves.

Susanne and I will be delighted if you post a review on Amazon or some other book site where you have an account and posting privileges. Maybe you can mention what kind of fiction you write, and explain which chapters you found most helpful and why.

Email me the link to your review, and I'll send you a free review copy (ebook) of one of my other Writer's Craft books. Let me know which one you would like: *Writing Fight Scenes, Writing Scary Scenes, The Word-Loss Diet, Writing About Magic, Writing About Villains, Writing Dark Stories, Euphonics For Writers, Writing Short Stories to Promote Your Novels, Twitter for Writers, Why Does My Book Not Sell? 20 Simple Fixes, Writing Vivid Settings, How To Train Your Cat To Promote Your Book, Writing Deep Point of View, Getting Book Reviews, Novel Revision Prompts, Writing Vivid Dialogue, Writing Vivid Characters, Writing Book Blurbs and Synopses, Writing Vivid Plots, Write Your Way Out Of Depression: Practical Self-Therapy For Creative Writers, Fantasy Writing Prompts, Horror Writing Prompts, Dr Rayne's Guide to Writerly Disorders.*

In some chapters, I've made suggestions for further study. You may want to choose one of those books for your review.

My email is contact@raynehall.com. Drop me a line if you've spotted any typos which have escaped the proof-reader's eagle eyes, or want to give me private feedback or have questions.

You can also contact me on Twitter: <u>https://twitter.com/RayneHall</u>. Tweet me that you've read this book, and I'll probably follow you back.

If you find this book helpful, it would be great if you could spread the word about it. Maybe you know other writers who would benefit.

I'm also adding an excerpt from another Writer's Craft Guide you may find useful: *Writing Vivid Emotions*. I hope you like it.

With best wishes for your writing success,

Rayne Hall

ABOUT THE AUTHORS

Rayne Hall is the author of over seventy books, mostly in the Fantasy, Horror and Historical fiction genres, as well as in non-fiction, including the bestselling series of blue Writer's Craft guides.

Many of her short stories and novels involve a strong love story plot, but none are in the Romance genre.

Many years ago, Rayne tried to pen Romance novels – but somehow the books always grew sinister during the writing. However innocuous the stories started, halfway through the plot she discovered that the hero was possessed by a demon, that the heroine was a vengeful serial killer, or that dismembered corpses were stowed under the bed where the couple were making love. She has accepted her calling, and now writes Horror instead of Romance.

After living in Germany, China, Mongolia, Nepal and Britain, Rayne has recently moved to Bulgaria. She enjoys reading, gardening, going for long walks and training her three cats.

Rayne's website is raynehall.com.

You can follow her on Twitter where she tweets cute photos of her cats and tips for writers: twitter.com/raynehall

Susanne McCarthy has been writing for many years – mostly Romance, with a little spice! For her, romance is the froth on the coffee of life. When real life is tough, the news full of disaster and dismay, what's wrong with a little fantasy, a little escapism?

Starting in 1986 with *A Long Way From Heaven*, she had twenty-five books published by Mills & Boon – some of them are still available on their website (though only as e-books).

www.millsandboon.co.uk/authors/p2828/Susanne-McCarthy

More recently she has begun publishing independently. You can find the links to these on her website. There are also a few short stories on there (and a little more about Susanne, if you're interested!)

www.susannemccarthy.com

Do let Susanne know what you think about her stuff – there's a comments link on her website. Or come over and chat on Twitter or Facebook.

ACKNOWLEDGEMENTS

I give sincere thanks to the beta readers and critiquers who read the draft chapters and offered valuable feedback: Anna Ereshkigal, Aedyn Brooks, Elise M Stone, Kathy Frost, Larisa Walk, Melissa Tacket, Juneta Key and Layo Osho.

The book cover is by Erica Syverson and Manuel Berbin. Julia Gibbs proofread the manuscript, and Eled Cernik formatted the book.

And finally, I say thank you to my cats Sulu (black adult), Yura (tortie kitten) and Janice (ginger kitten) who took turns snuggling on the desk between my arms and purring their approval as I typed.

Rayne Hall

I'd say thank you to my dog, a delinquent border terrier called Holly. But she insists on sharing my typing chair, leaving me to perch on about four inches of the edge. I'm sure J.K. Rowling doesn't have that problem.

Susanne McCarthy

EXCERPT FROM
WRITING VIVID EMOTIONS

CHAPTER 6

DESCRIPTIONS CONVEY MOOD

In this chapter, I'll show you how you can subtly convey how the PoV character feels, and at the same time manipulate the reader's emotions.

When you describe something, use words that evoke emotional connotations. Focus especially on verbs.

Here several sentences describing dusk. Each reflects a different emotion in the PoV and evokes a different mood in the reader.

Sunset gilded the horizon.

The sky bruised into night.

The sun dropped, taking the last remaining warmth with it.

The horizon throbbed crimson, then gentled to a soft pink.

Thick clouds hung on the horizon, and only a watery strip of orange peeked through.

The sun set, leaving a red-gashing wound between the earth and the sky.

The sky was sliding into dour night.

The day was already dying. Dusk hung like a purple mist.

The clouds at the horizon darkened. A sliver of the sinking sun glinted in their folds.

Sundown bloodied the horizon.

The sky flared up in hues of crimson and purple.

The last sliver of sunlight vanished from the sky.

Darkness came down like a hood.

The sun sank to rest behind the wagon track.

Within minutes, the fierce colours faded to pale.

Wind-ruffled pink clouds drifted along the horizon.

The sun slipped behind the dunes and cast a golden veil across their shifting shapes.

The sun painted a last, brilliant orange streak across the jagged mountain.

The sun died in streaks of gold and purple.

As you can see, there are many ways to describe a sunset. Obviously, not every one of these would suit every story and every writing style.

I've already used some of these in my novels, so if you want a sunset, don't copy my phrases but create your own mood-rich descriptions.

Here's another example. The PoV character sees another person who wears a gold choker around her neck.

Instead of simply stating

She wore a gold choker around her neck.

Try to convey how the PoV character feels about this woman, about the necklace, or about the situation in general. You might choose one of these:

A gold choker clawed at her neck.

A gold choker embraced her neck.

A gold choker caressed her neck.

A gold choker glinted around her neck.

A gold choker slithered around her neck.

A gold choker sparkled around her neck.

A gold choker snaked around her neck.

To convey or create positive emotions such as joy, hope and happiness, use positive verbs like *sparkle, dance, lap, skip, embrace, hug, shine, bloom, crown, caress.*

For dark moods and emotions, use verbs with negative connotations, such as *slash, rob, claw, stab, stump, steal, slither, scratch, dump, boil, scrape, squash, struggle, beg, clutch, grasp, devour, squeeze.*

WHAT NOT TO DO

Don't use in-your-face metaphors for descriptions. If the PoV character feels depressed, don't show heavy clouds in the sky. If she's desperate, don't show starving children in ragged clothes, and if she's happy, don't show a field of frolicking lambs. The effect would be melodramatic. Although melodrama has its uses in some kinds of fiction, most novels are better without it.

Beginners are prone to this mistake, especially when describing the weather. In novice-written stories it always rains when the character feels sad, and when she feels cheerful, the sun shines. In literary criticism, this is called a 'pathetic fallacy'.

For a subtler effect without melodrama, choose weather conditions, landscapes and objects which don't reflect the emotion – but evoke the mood through your word choices.

Your happy character may see ragged children on a litter-strewn pavement, and you can describe this in a positive way by using words *like play, fun, laugh, dance, skip.* An unhappy character may see a garden arch covered in roses, and through her filter of experience it's a depressing sight if you use words like *smother, cling, snake, droop.*

PROFESSIONAL TIP

Use descriptions conveying emotions to foreshadow future plot events and to hint at things you don't spell out.

Perhaps it's evening, and one of the characters says she has to go home to her husband. She says it in a subdued voice, and her eyes have lost their sparkle. The readers understand that this woman doesn't look forward to spending the evening with that man, but don't know what's wrong. If you now insert a description of the sunset – *The sky bruised into night* – the readers will grasp on a subconscious level that the husband is a brutal man whose violence she fears.

If you choose to try this professional-level technique in your fiction, apply it with a light brush, so that readers are not consciously aware of what you are doing.

ASSIGNMENTS

1. Does your work-in-progress (WiP) have a scene which takes place in the evening? Consider how the PoV character feels. Write a sentence describing the sunset (or dusk, lights-out, descending darkness or other evening feature) with words that convey his emotions. Use the list of examples in this chapter as inspiration, without copying them. If your WiP has no evening scene at all, write about sunrise or high noon instead.

2. In a scene you are planning or revising, identify the PoV character's main emotion. Now consider the time of the day and the weather, and visualise the surroundings. How do they look, viewed through the filter of how the PoV character feels?

CPSIA information can be obtained
at www.ICGtesting.com
Printed in the USA
LVHW052320080119
603245LV00021B/1022/P